Beyond the Campfire: Rving in National Parks Made Easy

A Traveler's Handbook for Unforgettable Adventures

Jordan Mitchell

Table of Contents

INTRODUCTION

Welcome to "Beyond the Campfire: RVing in National Parks Made Easy," a comprehensive traveler's handbook designed to transform your RV journey into unforgettable adventures amidst the breathtaking beauty of National Parks. This guide is your key to unlocking the full potential of RV travel, providing essential insights, practical tips, and expert advice to ensure a seamless and enriching experience.

In the vast expanse of nature, there's something truly magical about embarking on a road trip in the comfort of an RV, surrounded by the awe-inspiring landscapes of National Parks. Whether you're a seasoned RVer or a novice explorer, this book is crafted to be your trusted companion on the road, helping you navigate the ins and outs of RVing in some of the most remarkable natural settings on Earth.

As you turn the pages, you'll discover the art of choosing the perfect RV, packing essential gear, and understanding the intricate web of National Park regulations. We delve into the intricacies of planning your route, guiding you through the creation of a flexible itinerary that allows for spontaneous detours and unexpected discoveries. From campground etiquette to cooking delicious meals on the road, each chapter is designed to enhance your RV experience, making it not only enjoyable but also sustainable.

"Beyond the Campfire" is more than just a handbook – it's an invitation to connect with nature, immerse yourself in outdoor activities, and capture the essence of each National Park visit. With a focus on responsible travel, we explore ways to minimize your environmental impact, leaving these pristine landscapes as beautiful as you found them.

Whether you seek solitude in the wilderness, crave adventure on hiking trails, or simply want to savor the joy of the open road, this guide empowers you to craft your own unique and unforgettable RVing experience. So, fasten your seatbelt, embrace the freedom of the open road, and let "Beyond the Campfire" be your trusted guide to RVing in National Parks made easy. Your journey to extraordinary adventures begins here.

CHAPTER I

Choosing the Right RV

Types of RVs suitable for National Park adventures

To go on an RV journey throughout the tranquil landscapes of National Parks, it is necessary to seriously consider the type of recreational vehicle that is most suitable for your travel preferences and requirements. Every traveler can discover the ideal travel partner for their tour of National Parks thanks to the variety of available recreational vehicle (RV) alternatives. These RVs appeal to a variety of lifestyles and travel types.

Regarding excursions in national parks, the Class B motorhome, also frequently referred to as the camper van, is one of the most popular accommodations. Because of their small size and maneuverability, these vehicles offer a mix of comfort and efficiency, making them perfect for traversing the frequently winding and tight roads within National Parks. A self-contained experience is provided by Class B motorhomes, distinguished from more oversized recreational vehicles (RVs) by amenities such as a kitchenette, bathing facilities, and a comfortable sleeping area. Because of their smaller size, they also provide more excellent choices when selecting camping areas within the park, especially those sections with size restrictions.

A compelling choice is available in the form of the Class C motorhome for individuals who want more space and conveniences. These cars often have a distinctive sleeping section that is located over the cab, offering additional sleeping accommodations without compromising the living space available inside the vehicle. Motorhomes in the Class C category typically have a bathroom, a kitchen, and suitable living and sleeping quarters. Their size is reasonable, which makes them ideal for exploring national parks. They offer a decent compromise between mobility and creature comforts, making them suitable for such exploration.

The Class A motorhome may be the best option for you if you're seeking a home-on-wheels equipped with all the conveniences of contemporary living. These recreational vehicles (RVs) are comparable to mobile apartments in terms of their spaciousness and level of comfort and offer a high level of convenience. Even though Class A motorhomes are often larger and less maneuverable than their competitors, developments in RV design and technology have produced more maneuverable versions ideal for travel in national parks. Families and individuals looking for a deluxe experience amid nature will find these accommodations a good choice because of their spacious interiors.

People who would instead tow their lodgings by themselves can use travel trailers and fifth wheels as an alternative. The hitch used to pull travel trailers is usually attached to the back of the vehicle, but the hitch used to remove fifth wheels is a specialty attachment installed in the bed of a pickup truck. Both choices provide a living room separate from the rest of the house, enabling greater flexibility when it comes to parking and exploring national parks. Travel trailers and fifth wheels are available in a wide range of sizes and floor designs, making them suitable for groups of people traveling alone, in pairs, or with children. Because of their detachable nature, they provide mobility that is only sometimes attainable with motorhomes. This independence allows you to set up camp and tour the park in a separate vehicle.

Pop-up and truck campers are two examples of alternatives that are robust and adaptable, and they may be appealing to individuals who are more experienced in off-roading and adventure. In addition to being lightweight and simple to pull, pop-up campers offer a comfortable sleeping area with canvas walls that can be raised to create a more open and spacious atmosphere. On the other hand, a truck camper is attached to the bed of a pickup truck and provides a living space that is both compact and functional. The design of these choices makes it possible to have a more immersive camping experience while still providing needed utilities, making them an excellent choice for individuals looking to feel more physically connected to the natural world.

When planning a trip to a national park, it is vital to consider a number of elements, including size, weight, and maneuverability, regardless of the type of selected recreational vehicle. In many national parks, there are limitations placed on the length and size of cars permitted to travel on particular routes and be parked in specific campgrounds. Consequently, selecting a recreational vehicle (RV) by the park's regulations guarantees a smooth and pleasurable journey.

In conclusion, the wide variety of available recreational vehicle (RV) options makes it possible for every tourist to locate the ideal vehicle for seeing the natural treasures found in national parks on their trip. There is a recreational vehicle (RV) that is specifically designed to enhance your experience in National Parks, regardless of whether you prefer the compact convenience of a Class B motorhome, the roomy elegance of a Class A motorhome, the towable flexibility of travel trailers and fifth wheels, or the adventurous spirit of pop-up and truck campers. As you set out on your tour, the perfect recreational vehicle (RV) transforms from being a means of transportation into a home on wheels, allowing you to have a more profound connection with the breathtaking landscapes that are what make National Parks so remarkable.

Factors to consider when selecting an RV

It is a crucial decision that can considerably affect your journey's enjoyment, and choosing the correct recreational vehicle (RV) for your travel experiences is one critical option. The process of selecting a decision should be guided by a number of important considerations as you investigate the vast selection of recreational vehicles that are currently available on the market. This will ensure that the RV you select is suitable for your requirements, preferences, and the kinds of travel experiences that you are looking for.

The size and layout of an RV are two of the most important factors to take into consideration while choosing one. There is a wide range of sizes available for recreational vehicles (RVs), from modest camper vans to huge Class A motorhomes. The size of the recreational vehicle (RV) is a significant factor in determining its usability, the simplicity with which it may be parked, and the accessibility of various camping locations. RVs that are smaller, such as camper vans and Class B motorhomes, provide more freedom when traveling on roads that are narrower and while camping in campgrounds that have size limits. Larger Class A motorhomes, on the other hand, offer a more significant amount of living space and facilities, making them suited for individuals who place considerable importance on comfort and elegance. It is crucial to find a balance between size and comfort, making sure that your selected recreational vehicle (RV) satisfies your spatial requirements while still enabling you to maneuver across a variety of terrains, including the occasionally complex landscapes that are found within national parks.

In the process of selecting a recreational vehicle (RV), budgetary concerns play a crucial role. There is a broad range of variation in the price of recreational vehicles due to a variety of criteria including size, brand, age, and features. In order to reduce the number of possibilities available and avoid going over budget, it is advisable to establish a reasonable budget before beginning the search. The purchase price is not the only thing that needs to be taken into consideration; continuing costs such as maintenance, fuel, campground
fees, and prospective storage charges should also be taken into account. Other people may discover that a more budget-friendly alternative, such as a travel trailer or camper van, better meets their financial restraints without compromising on the whole travel experience. While some people may be tempted to the appeal of opulent Class A motorhomes, others may discover that a camper van or travel trailer works better for them.

When selecting an RV, it is of the utmost importance to have a solid understanding of your personal travel tastes and lifestyle. Take into consideration how you intend to utilize the vehicle; will it serve as a weekend getaway, a home on wheels for extended road trips, or a residence that you will use on a permanent basis? It is crucial to consider the intended use when selecting the essential facilities and features. If you are someone who enjoys activities outside and wants to spend the most of your time outdoors, a more basic recreational vehicle (RV) that has minimal amenities might be sufficient for you. If, on the other hand, you would rather have a more independent experience that includes all of the conveniences of home, then a fully-equipped Class A or Class C motorhome would be a better option for you that meets your needs. Consider your chosen mode of transportation and the kinds of things you take pleasure in doing in order to find a recreational vehicle (RV) that will improve your experience as a whole.

In the event that you decide to go with a fifth wheel or a travel trailer, another essential aspect to take into consideration is the towing capacity of your vehicle. Towing capacities vary from recreational vehicle to recreational vehicle, and it is vital to ensure that the weight of the RV is compatible with the towing capacity of your car. It is possible that failure to do so will result in safety concerns as well as significant damage to your vehicle. In addition, it is essential to have a thorough understanding of the physics of towing, including the impact on fuel efficiency and driving stability, in order to have a straightforward and stress-free experience when towing. In the event that you do not already possess a suitable towing vehicle, as part of your decision-making process, you should take into consideration the purchase price as well as the many factors involved.

The level of comfort and convenience that you feel throughout your travels is strongly impacted by the facilities and features that are provided by a recreational vehicle (RV). There is a large variety of amenities that may be included in contemporary recreational vehicles (RVs), such as full kitchens, baths, entertainment systems, and slide-out sections that increase the amount of living space available. Nevertheless, it is necessary to prioritize features according to the requirements that are unique to you. It may be essential to have a kitchen that is well-equipped if you intend to prepare complex meals while you are traveling. Those who place a high value on getting a restful night's sleep should place a high priority on the quality of their sleeping arrangements and bedding. When it comes to arranging and stowing goods while traveling, it is necessary to have storage space available, both inside and outside of the recreational vehicle (RV). Ensure that your chosen recreational vehicle (RV) is compatible with your lifestyle by taking into consideration your daily routines, preferences, and essential characteristics.

During the process of selecting an RV, it is essential to not overlook the maintenance requirements. For long-term ownership satisfaction, it is necessary to have a thorough awareness of the maintenance requirements that are associated with the various types of recreational vehicles (RVs). Motorhomes that fall into the Class A and Class C categories, for example, may have more complicated systems and components, which necessitate routine maintenance and may bring about increased repair expenses. On the other hand, recreational vehicles (RVs) that are more simplistic, such as camper vans and travel trailers, perhaps have fewer components, which makes maintenance simpler. Determine whether you are comfortable performing maintenance tasks on your own or whether you are willing to invest in professional services, and then select a recreational vehicle that is compatible with your preferences and capabilities regarding maintenance.
It is also essential to take into consideration the age of the recreational vehicle. A brand-new recreational vehicle (RV) comes with a higher price tag, despite the fact that it has the most recent features and technology. On the other hand, getting a used recreational vehicle (RV) can result in cost savings; but, it may also come with wear and tear or systems that are very old. When purchasing a secondhand recreational vehicle (RV), it is essential to perform a thorough inspection and receive a comprehensive history. It is crucial to establish a

balance between the limits of the budget and the need for modern amenities, making sure that the RV that is selected satisfies both the financial and functional criteria you have decided upon.

In this day and age of sustainability, it is becoming increasingly crucial to take into consideration the influence that your choice of RV will have on the environment. In general, recreational vehicles that are smaller and more fuel-efficient have a smaller environmental footprint than larger versions that consume a lot of petrol. Some manufacturers of recreational vehicles are also including environmentally friendly elements into their designs, such as solar panels and appliances that are efficient in their use of energy. It is possible to contribute to ethical and sustainable travel habits by selecting a recreational vehicle (RV) that matches with your environmental ideals. This will help you minimize the influence that you have on the natural beauty of the places that you visit.

As a conclusion, choosing the appropriate recreational vehicle (RV) for your excursions in national parks requires careful consideration of a number of different criteria, each of which plays an integral part in determining the nature of your trip experience. The decision-making process takes into account a variety of factors, including size, affordability, lifestyle, towing capability, amenities, maintenance requirements, age, and environmental impact. When you take the time to thoroughly evaluate your specific requirements and preferences in each of these areas, you will be able to locate a recreational vehicle (RV) that not only satisfies your expectations but also enhances the pleasure and comfort of your journey through the breathtaking landscapes of national parks. Over time, the perfect recreational vehicle (RV) transforms into more than just a means of transportation; it transforms into your home on wheels, allowing you to have a more profound connection with the natural world and to create experiences that will last a lifetime.

Tips for renting or buying the perfect RV for your needs

To choose the ideal recreational vehicle (RV), whether for a short vacation or a long road trip, it is necessary to consider several different aspects. There are a lot of people who travel, and the question comes down to whether they should rent or buy an RV. Before choosing a choice that suits your travel requirements and tastes, it is essential to have a thorough understanding of the nuances of both options, as each comes with its unique set of benefits and factors to consider.

People looking for flexibility and variety in their vacation experiences may find that renting a recreational vehicle (RV) is an appealing alternative. You can select the style and size of recreational vehicle (RV) that is most suitable for your current trip without committing to ownership for an extended period. Rental options range from camper vans that are small and compact to motorhomes that are large and roomy, making it possible to accommodate a wide variety of travel preferences. This flexibility is especially beneficial for people who only travel sometimes and who may want to avoid the hassle of owning and maintaining an RV when it is not being used.

Before committing to a purchase, renting a recreational vehicle (RV) allows you to test various types and sizes, one of the most significant advantages. By gaining this hands-on experience, you can choose which features and layouts most suit your preferences and individual requirements. Renting a recreational vehicle (RV) is a low-risk introduction to the world of recreational vehicles that allows first-time RVers to learn the ropes without the financial and long-term commitment associated with ownership.

The convenience of having a well-maintained and serviced recreational vehicle (RV) while you are on your journey is yet another perk of renting. Most of the time, rental companies ensure that their cars are in good shape. This helps to reduce the risk of unanticipated breakdowns or maintenance difficulties occurring while you are on your trip. Because of this, it can be incredibly reassuring for travelers who might need more technical understanding or the inclination to manage RV maintenance independently.

One further realistic option for individuals who do not possess a suitable towing vehicle for particular types of recreational vehicles (RVs), such as travel trailers or fifth wheels, is to rent those vehicles. Delivery and setup services are frequently provided by rental firms, enabling you to enjoy the experience of renting a recreational vehicle (RV) without needing specialist towing equipment. Individuals interested in experiencing the RV lifestyle but still need to prepare to make the financial commitment to purchase a full-fledged towing vehicle may find this a game-changer.

On the other hand, purchasing a recreational vehicle appeals to individuals interested in long-term ownership since it enables a sense of familiarity and customization. Your recreational vehicle (RV) transforms into a personal place you can adapt and decorate according to your preferences, transforming it into a home away from home. Additionally, having a recreational vehicle (RV) avoids the need to continuously become comfortable with different cars, which results in a travel experience that is consistent and predictable because of the RV.

When considering whether or not to purchase a recreational vehicle (RV), the frequency of use is one of the most important factors to consider. Owning a recreational vehicle (RV) could be a more cost-effective option in the long term if you want to take several RV trips during the year. On the other hand, rental may be a more cost-effective alternative if you only sometimes travel with your recreational vehicle (RV). This will save you from recurring ownership expenses, such as insurance, maintenance, and storage.

The ability to hit the road at a moment's notice is one of the benefits of having a recreational vehicle (RV) for individuals who enjoy impromptu vacations. Consequently, you will no longer be required to book in advance, enabling you to enjoy a more adaptable travel schedule. A further advantage of RV ownership is the ability to personalize your recreational vehicle (RV) to meet specific requirements, such as changes that are friendly to pets or accessibility features. This allows you to ensure that your RV is in perfect harmony with your way of life.

When purchasing a recreational vehicle (RV), it is vital to undertake extensive research to choose a model that satisfies your particular requirements. If applicable, consider aspects such as the vehicle's size, layout, amenities, and towing capacity. To guarantee the RV's quality and condition, it is essential to purchase from a dealer with a good reputation or from a private seller who can be trusted. Before making a purchase, a thorough inspection is recommended, including a check of the mechanical and electrical systems. This will allow for the identification of any potential problems that may exist.

Leasing a recreational vehicle (RV) is a reasonable alternative for individuals looking for a compromise between renting and owning a car. Through leasing, one can obtain a long-term commitment without making the entire investment required for ownership. Leasing combines aspects of both renting and buying. Those who want the benefits of extended use without the long-term commitment can find a balance in leasing, even though it comes with certain restrictions, such as mileage limits and the possibility of excessive wear and tear costs.

It is essential to have a comprehensive grasp of RV ownership or rental cost, which goes beyond the original price or rental fee, regardless of whether the RV is being rented, leased, or purchased. It is essential to consider other costs like insurance, fees assessed by campgrounds, fuel, maintenance, and probable storage costs. Being aware of these expenditures enables you to create a more realistic budget and guarantees that the option you select is in line with your financial capabilities.

Regardless of whether you decide to rent or buy a recreational vehicle (RV), some basic guidelines can help you choose the RV that is best suited to meet your requirements. Initially and most importantly, it is necessary to determine the number of passengers and the amount of living space required for a comfortable journey. To ensure that the recreational vehicle (RV) is suitable for your lifestyle, it is essential to consider aspects such as sleeping arrangements, kitchen facilities, and bathroom amenities.

The capacity of your car to pull a trailer or fifth wheel is another essential factor to consider if you intend to pull a travel trailer or fifth wheel. Ensure that your vehicle can safely tow the RV of your choice by considering its weight, braking capabilities, and overall compatibility with towing. When you fail to match the towing capability of your vehicle with the weight of the recreational vehicle (RV), it can lead to significant safety hazards and damage to both the RV and the car being used to pull it.

Test-driving is a vital activity for individuals who are considering purchasing a motorized recreational vehicle. For a better understanding of the handling, visibility, and overall driving experience, you should get behind the wheel. Considering how comfortable you are using the RV to navigate through different terrains is essential since this will affect how enjoyable and easy your trips are. Furthermore, paying attention to characteristics such as driving assistance, ergonomic design, and general mobility is essential.

Before renting, it is essential to carefully read the rental agreement to become familiar with the terms, conditions, and potential fees. Ensure you know all the specifics, including the mileage allotment, insurance coverage, and any restrictions on trip destinations. Before finishing the rental agreement, you must ensure that any issues you have are addressed and clarified. Some rental businesses may have specific laws about pets, smoking, and off-road travel.

Purchasers must have a thorough check from a certified mechanic, regardless of whether they are acquiring a new or used vehicle. This process assists in identifying any existing concerns or prospective future problems, which eventually enables decisions to be made in an informed manner. Additionally, it is recommended to research the reputation of the RV manufacturer, read reviews written by other owners, and consider aspects such as the resale value and the warranty choices available.

It would help if you constantly considered the long-term consequences of your decision, regardless of whether you choose to rent or own a home. Evaluating your dedication to the RV lifestyle, the number of times you travel, and the financial limits you face is essential. Your RV trip will be pleasurable and suited to your travel style if you have a good awareness of your tastes and requirements. This will help you find the most suitable option for your needs.

To summarize, choosing whether to rent or purchase a recreational vehicle (RV) is a crucial milestone in the evolution of your travel experiences. There are various benefits associated with each alternative, and the selection of one is contingent upon the individual's preferences, the frequency of travel, and the financial considerations involved. Regardless of whether you choose to rent because of its flexibility, to purchase because of its long-term commitment, or to lease because of its middle ground, the most important thing is to be sure that your choice aligns with your lifestyle and travel objectives. You can confidently select the ideal recreational vehicle (RV) for your requirements if you carefully evaluate your requirements, conduct extensive research, and consider a variety of aspects, including size, amenities, towing capacity, and overall cost. This will allow you to go on a journey filled with beautiful experiences.

CHAPTER II

Essential Gear and Equipment

Camping gear checklist

Preparing for a camping adventure requires careful planning and consideration of the essential gear to ensure a comfortable and enjoyable outdoor experience. Having the appropriate camping equipment can significantly impact your ability to traverse the outdoors and make lifelong memories successfully. A thorough camping gear checklist is essential to ensure you're prepared for every eventuality, regardless of experience level with outdoor activities.

The most essential item on any list of camping supplies is shelter. Your camping style and the surrounding conditions will determine the kind of shelter you select. When going on a typical tent camping trip, ensure your tent is sturdy and big enough for the number of people in your company. When choosing a tent, consider weather resistance, durability, and ease of setup. Bring a ground tarp as well for additional protection from the cold and moisture. In place of conventional tents, hammocks with rainfly attachments provide a cozy and lightweight option for individuals looking for a more straightforward and lightweight solution.

An additional essential item on a camping checklist is sleeping gear. It would help to have a high-quality sleeping bag appropriate for the temperatures predicted at your campground. When choosing a sleeping bag, consider the climate and aspects like weight, shape, and compressibility. A sleeping pad or air mattress also improves comfort and provides insulation against the cold ground. Lightweight, compact, inflatable pads are perfect for hikes, while thicker air mattresses offer a more plush camping experience.

Because the weather outside might be unpredictable, packing for a camping trip requires careful consideration of clothing. Bring a variety of layers, such as moisture-wicking base layers, insulating mid-layers, and waterproof outer layers, to accommodate temperature swings. Remember to bring additional socks and underwear and sturdy hiking boots or shoes appropriate for the terrain. Your camping gear should also include gloves for colder weather, a beanie for warmth, and a hat for sun protection. A trustworthy rain jacket is also essential for keeping dry during unforeseen downpours.

A camping equipment checklist must include food and cooking supplies because they directly affect your ability to stay nourished while traveling. To prepare hot meals, you'll need lightweight, portable cooking equipment, like a grill or camping stove. Bring plates, cups, silverware, and a set of sturdy cooking tools, pans, and pots. An ice-pack cooler or a portable camping refrigerator can keep perishable food products fresh longer. To expedite cooking and save waste, prepare certain meals ahead of time. Bring non-perishable snacks on walks or other outdoor activities to replenish your energy quickly.

Staying hydrated and using water is essential in the great outdoors, and packing appropriately guarantees a fun and safe camping trip. You'll need a dependable water filtration system or purification tablets to make water from natural sources, such as rivers or lakes, safe to drink. Bring enough water bottles or hydration packs to stay hydrated during your camping adventure. It would help if you planned with the availability of water sources at your campground in mind.

When camping, having navigational aids and lights is crucial for your convenience and safety. You can ensure you stay on the correct path and traverse the trails with a trustworthy GPS device, a compass, and an extensive map of the area. Headlamps or flashlights with spare batteries are essential for lighting purposes both within and outside the campsite, especially for emergencies or nocturnal activities. Think about carrying rechargeable or solar-powered lights to lessen your influence on the environment and reduce the disposable batteries you use.

Safety and first aid supplies should always be considered when creating a camping gear checklist. A well-stocked first aid bag with bandages, antiseptic wipes, painkillers, and any required prescription prescriptions is crucial for treating minor wounds and diseases. Add extras like a multipurpose tool, a fire starter, and a repair kit for your camping equipment. To protect oneself from the weather, use sunscreen and insect repellent. In an emergency, a whistle or signaling device can be helpful. Before camping, familiarize yourself with emergency protocols and basic first aid techniques.

The luxuries of your campsite can make your camping trip even more enjoyable. At the campsite or around the campfire, foldable or portable camping chairs offer a cozy seating choice. A portable table can be used to cook and serve food, engage in recreational activities, or provide a practical surface for various tasks. For longer excursions or places without access to services, think about packing a portable camping shower, enabling you to take care of your hygiene while enjoying the great outdoors.

Though optional, entertainment and relaxation equipment can make a camping trip pleasurable. To spend time at the campsite, bring a musical instrument, a deck of cards, or a good book when birdwatching or studying animals. Binoculars are helpful for a deeper understanding of the natural world. A comfy hammock or camping chair offers a warm place to unwind and take in the tranquil beauty of nature.

When going camping, it's essential to consider the environment to ensure sustainable and responsible outdoor activities. Bring reusable and environmentally friendly supplies like reusable plates, cups, and silverware to reduce waste. Please respect the environment and leave it as pure as you found it, dispose of rubbish appropriately, and adhere to the Leave No Trace philosophy. When cleaning, use biodegradable soap and stay on designated routes to prevent upsetting wildlife. To guarantee that your actions keep with the local conservation efforts, familiarize yourself with the rules and restrictions unique to the camping area.

In conclusion, the secret to a successful and pleasurable outdoor experience is a well-prepared camping gear checklist. Every item on the checklist is essential for your camping trip to be comfortable, safe, and convenient. Whether you're an experienced camper or a novice, ensuring you have everything you need for a successful trip includes thinking through the specific needs of your trip in advance. These include clothing, sleeping gear, food, and cooking equipment, water and hydration tools, navigational and lighting aids, safety and first aid supplies, campsite comforts, and optional entertainment items. You can make enduring memories and develop a closer bond with the surrounding natural beauty by packing sensibly and ethically.

Safety equipment for RV travel

When traveling, it is crucial to make sure that you, your passengers, and your recreational vehicle (RV) are all safe. Preparing a journey necessitates including complete safety equipment due to the specific obstacles and considerations associated with RV travel. The appropriate safety gear can make a big difference in your ability to drive confidently and worry-free, from preventive measures to emergency response tools.

An essential safety factor when traveling in an RV is the significance of regular maintenance. Frequent inspections of the car's vital components, such as the engine, tires, brakes, and fluid levels, can assist in finding possible problems early on and fixing them. Ensure that every part of the RV, from the plumbing to the roof, is in good operating order by thoroughly checking the outside and inside before every trip. In addition to extending the life and functionality of your RV, routine maintenance lowers the likelihood of malfunctions while traveling.

Because of the unique demands that the weight and size of recreational vehicles make on their tires, tire safety is an essential part of RV travel. Ensure your tires are correctly inflated, have even wear, and have enough tread depth to prioritize maintenance. Get a high-quality tire pressure monitoring system (TPMS) to get real-time notifications about tire pressure and temperature. An RV blowout can have serious repercussions, so having a TPMS early warning system enables you to take care of tire problems before they become harmful.

RV safety largely depends on emergency readiness, and a fully functional emergency pack is crucial. Basic first aid materials like bandages, antiseptic wipes, painkillers, and any required prescription drugs should be included in the kit. Add extras like a fire extinguisher, a multipurpose tool, a flashlight with extra batteries, and an essential tool kit. Learn how to utilize the items in the emergency kit to prepare you to handle unforeseen circumstances while driving.

Fire safety is crucial since an RV is a compact place where a small fire can quickly grow. Put carbon monoxide and smoke detectors in strategic locations throughout the RV, and ensure they are working correctly by regularly testing and replacing the batteries. Keep a fire extinguisher beside the bedroom and one readily available in the kitchen. Provide a strategy for evacuation to all passengers and let them know where the closest exits and assembly areas are. Do frequent fire drills to ensure everyone is aware of emergency protocols.

RV travel frequently entails visiting isolated locations, so having communication equipment is essential for remaining in touch and requesting help when necessary. Purchase a dependable communication device, such as a satellite phone or an excellent two-way radio, especially if you're going somewhere with spotty cellphone service. Ensure your phone has the apps you need, like weather updates and navigation, and always have a backup power source on you, such as a solar-powered or a portable charger, to keep your gadgets charged.

A thorough inventory of safety equipment should include tools for leveling and stabilizing an RV. The uneven ground might impair the RV's stability, which can impact comfort and safety. Carry ramps or leveling blocks to ensure the RV is parked on a level, solid surface. RVs can be further stabilized when parked by adding stabilizing jacks or stabilizer bars, stopping the vehicle from needlessly rocking or swaying.

Knowing the RV's weight restrictions and ensuring it is correctly loaded and balanced is essential to its safety. Reduced maneuverability, longer stopping distances, and more system stress can result from overloading an RV. When pulling a trailer, use a weight distribution hitch and sway control system, and appropriately distribute the load within the RV. Ensure the RV stays within its designated weight restrictions by routinely checking the weight distribution.

Roadside assistance and essential repair tools should be included in the safety equipment for RV travel, in addition to preventive measures. A complete tool kit that provides pliers, screwdrivers, wrenches, and other necessary equipment lets you handle minor problems while traveling. Bring an extra tire and the equipment needed to change a flat, and become familiar with the RV's handbook to solve typical issues.

While traveling in an RV, weather conditions might present difficulties. Therefore, safety equipment should be chosen with any weather-related concerns in mind. Consider bringing tire chains in the event of snow or ice, and know how well the RV handles cold weather. Fit the RV with weather-appropriate wipers and make sure the air conditioning and heating work properly. Keep up with weather forecasts and be ready to adjust your travel schedule in case of extreme weather, such as strong winds or storms.

A vital component of traveling in an RV is driving safely, and having the appropriate gear can improve your road trip experience in general. Install extra safety mirrors to increase visibility, especially when hauling a trailer. For assistance with parking and to keep an eye on blind areas, consider purchasing a rearview camera system. Driving can be made more stable by reducing the impact of oncoming traffic and crosswinds using anti-sway bars or steering stabilizers.

Maintaining local traffic laws and regulations is crucial for RV safety, particularly when traveling over national or international boundaries. Learn the necessary turning and braking distances and other RV-specific driving methods. Take stops and rotate driving duties with other competent and licensed passengers to avoid getting tired on lengthy rides.

RVs frequently utilize propane for refrigeration, heating, and cooking; therefore, safety precautions should be taken to avoid mishaps. Install a propane leak detector within the recreational vehicle to give early alerts during a gas leak. Make sure all connections are safe and that propane equipment is maintained correctly. When traveling or storing the RV, use the propane shut-off valve that you are familiar with where it is located.

Wildlife encounters are possible when camping in isolated locations. Thus, precautions should be taken to reduce dangers. Store food safely in lockable compartments or bear-resistant containers to avoid drawing wildlife to your campground. Respect animals' natural habitats and be informed of any local wildlife laws or policies. Avoid feeding wildlife and maintain a safe distance from them, as interactions with people can harm humans and animals.

In summary, safety gear for recreational vehicles (RVs) includes an extensive array of devices and precautions intended to improve passengers' general security and welfare. Every part, from regular maintenance to emergency readiness, is essential to reducing hazards and handling obstacles that may appear while driving, and putting safety first guarantees that your RV trip will be not only fun but safe and stress-free, regardless of how experienced you are as a traveler. With the appropriate safety gear and preparation, you may confidently drive across broad spaces and make lifelong experiences.

Must-have accessories for a comfortable trip

When setting out on a journey, whether a road trip, a camping excursion, or an extended vacation, consider the accessories that might boost comfort and convenience along the route. When you have the appropriate accessories, a journey may go from ordinary to extraordinary. This is true regardless of whether you are traveling in a camper, a car, or an RV. This essay will discuss various essential accessories for a comfortable and enjoyable travel experience. We will cover critical areas such as organization and storage, technology and entertainment, comfort and relaxation, safety and convenience, and backpacking and camping equipment.

Organization and storage accessories are essential for keeping things in order and maximizing the space available on a journey. The use of packing cubes is quite beneficial since they allow for the tidy organization of supplies and clothing within luggage, reducing clutter and making it easier to find goods. Toiletry organizers hung on the wall are space-saving and offer handy storage for personal care items. They make accessing these items easy while maintaining a clean and organized bathroom space. Over-the-seat organizers are convenient since they allow for the storage of travel necessities within easy reach. These necessities include snacks, water bottles, and electronic gadgets, readily available when traveling.

An essential factor that contributes to the overall satisfaction of a trip is the presence of various technological and entertainment equipment. Installing a dependable car phone mount allows for hands-free communication and keeps navigation programs accessible, contributing to a more secure driving experience. Having portable chargers and power banks to keep electronic devices charged is vital. This will ensure that mobile devices like smartphones, tablets, and other electronic devices continue functioning correctly throughout the journey. Using noise-canceling headphones creates a quiet environment that enables travelers to listen to music, podcasts, or audiobooks without being distracted by the noise in the surrounding environment.

Accessories that offer comfort and relaxation are indispensable for making long journeys enjoyable. Imagine nestling into a memory foam travel pillow that cradles your neck, providing comfort and support, perfect for naps or extended periods of sitting. Envision wrapping yourself in a lightweight, compact travel blanket, offering warmth and coziness during chilly evenings or while traveling by airplane. Picture an impromptu stop in a scenic spot where you can unfurl a portable hammock, providing a comfortable suspended seat for soaking in nature's beauty or simply unwinding in the great outdoors.

Convenience and safety accessories are not just add-ons; they're essential for ensuring the well-being of passengers on the road. Imagine facing a minor injury or illness during your journey; a compact first aid kit with necessary medical materials becomes a necessity, not a luxury. Car emergency kits, with essential equipment and supplies, are your lifeline during unplanned breakdowns or mishaps. They ensure you're ready for any unexpected obstacles. Navigating dark locations, like campgrounds or unfamiliar accommodations, can take time and effort. But with keychain flashlights, you're not just increasing safety and visibility; you're buying peace of mind.

Outdoor and camping gear additions are designed to cater to individuals who enjoy spending time in the great outdoors when they are traveling. Providing a comfortable seating choice for outdoor activities or leisure by the campfire, portable camping chairs are lightweight and foldable, making them ideal for camping accommodations. It is easy to use collapsible water bottles since they allow you to stay hydrated while saving room when they are not in use. Camping excursions and picnics can be elevated to a more gastronomic level by adding portable grills or camping stoves, making it possible to prepare food outside.

In conclusion, the selection of essential accessories for a comfortable journey comprises a wide range of things designed to meet various requirements and tastes. These accessories, whether geared toward organization and storage, technology and entertainment, comfort and relaxation, safety and convenience, or gear for camping and outdoor activities, all add to an improved travel experience. A well-prepared traveler armed with the appropriate accessories can negotiate the challenges of the journey with ease and cherish the moments that make travel a memorable and delightful pursuit. A straightforward journey can be transformed into a well-rounded and pleasant exploration of the world with the help of these accessories, which become our reliable companions as we embark on our travels.

CHAPTER III

Navigating National Park Regulations

Understanding park rules and regulations

To engage in outdoor leisure that is both responsible and pleasurable, it is essential to comprehend and maintain compliance with the rules and regulations that govern the park. Parks are beloved natural settings that provide opportunities for relaxation, adventure, and connection with nature. Parks are at several levels, including national, state, and local. Parks, on the other hand, set laws and regulations that control the behavior and activities of visitors to facilitate the preservation of these habitats and to guarantee the visitors' safety and well-being. This essay investigates the necessity of understanding and obeying park rules. The study delves into why these laws are in place, the common types of regulations encountered in parks, the penalties of rule infractions, and how visitors may contribute to preserving these unique natural areas.

In addition to being places of scenic beauty and cultural significance, parks are also places of biodiversity. Activities like hiking, camping, picnics, and seeing animals can be enjoyed in the areas they provide for outdoor activities. The park's management establishes rules and regulations that control various aspects of visitor behavior to protect the natural integrity of these regions and ensure that all visitors have a positive experience. Not only are these regulations intended to safeguard the natural and cultural elements that are included inside the park, but they are also intended to guarantee the safety and enjoyment of every visitor.

One of the most common types of park rules is concerned with preserving the natural environment. Guidelines on how to utilize trails, engage with wildlife, and dispose of rubbish could be included in these rules. Trails are established to limit tourists' influence on delicate ecosystems to prevent habitat disturbance and soil erosion. This ensures that visitors stay on specified tracks the entire time they are there. Wildlife interaction laws frequently emphasize the importance of maintaining a safe distance from the animals to protect both the animals and the people visiting. The proper disposal of waste is of the utmost importance, and many parks have adopted the "Leave No Trace" philosophy, which encourages visitors to carry away all of their rubbish and reduce their impact on the environment.

The restrictions governing safety are yet another essential component of park guidelines. The purpose of these regulations is to lessen the likelihood of mishaps and unexpected situations, guaranteeing that guests can have pleasure in their time spent in the park without jeopardizing their health. Some parks, for instance, have regulations that state that swimming is only permitted in specific locations. There are lifeguards to ensure the water's safety. Open flames, such as campfires, are subject to regulations to forestall the occurrence of wildfires and safeguard the parks' ecosystems and visitors. Understanding and adhering to safety laws is a significant factor in ensuring everyone has a happy and secure experience.

Guidelines about visitor conduct have been set to cultivate a polite and harmonious atmosphere within the park. The noise levels, policies regarding pets, and appropriate behavior toward other guests are some of the topics that are frequently contained under these rules. The purpose of noise laws is to preserve the peace of natural areas, allowing visitors to enjoy nature's sounds without being disturbed. The pet policies can vary, but they typically include limits on particular routes and leash requirements to protect both the wildlife and other visitors involved. Respecting other people who are visiting the park by exhibiting a polite and courteous disposition assures that everyone will be able to take pleasure in the park experience.

Several parks strongly emphasize the preservation of historical and cultural information, particularly those parks with historical sites or cultural significance. The rules that govern these regions frequently emphasize the importance of ensuring that objects, constructions, or archeological sites are not disturbed. To protect the cultural legacy for future generations, visitors are strongly recommended to refrain from removing or defacing any objects on these sites. The historical and cultural significance of the park can be preserved through the conservation of these rules, which should be understood and respected.

The gravity of the infringement and the particular regulations in place can impact the consequences that individuals face when they violate park laws. As a consequence of minor infractions, such as failing to dispose of trash appropriately, warnings or fines may be issued. In the event of more severe violations, such as destroying natural features or historical objects, criminal charges and significant penalties may be brought against responsible parties. The enforcement of these laws is the responsibility of park rangers and personnel, and their duty extends beyond implementing punitive measures. In addition to this, they function as educators, advising visitors on appropriate behavior and assisting them in comprehending the reasoning behind specific rules.

Rule infractions have repercussions beyond the imposition of personal sanctions; they also affect the park's general health and capacity to remain sustainable. The damage that is done to the environment, whether it is done intentionally or accidentally, can have long-lasting impacts on ecosystems. Tourists can contribute to soil erosion by going off official paths or trails that need better maintenance. This can hurt the quality of water and the plant life in the area. The disturbance of animals can result in changes in behavior and population, affecting the delicate balance within the ecosystem. Irreparable harm can be caused to priceless artifacts and locations if the regulations governing the protection of historical and cultural heritage are broken.

Understanding and adhering to the park's rules is not only a moral and ethical requirement but also contributes to a more considerable conservation effort. The preservation of natural beauty, biodiversity, and cultural heritage is the primary objective of parks through their operations. A significant contribution to the achievement of these conservation objectives is made by visitors who observe the restrictions. To actively engage in the care of the park, visitors are required to stay on trails designated for them, dispose of rubbish responsibly, and respect both the wildlife and the cultural monuments.

Educational activities are vital in encouraging visitors to become more aware of and knowledgeable about park regulations. It is common practice for parks to give visitors instructional materials, signage, and guided programs to educate them on the significance of adhering to laws and the reasoning behind particular regulations. A deeper appreciation for the natural world and a sense of duty for its protection can be fostered through interpretive centers and activities guided by rangers. These activities provide vital insights into the park's ecological, historical, and cultural significance.

Participation from the community is crucial in fostering responsible park use, which goes beyond the realm of formal instruction. Local communities, conservation organizations, and park enthusiasts can work together to increase awareness about the significance of ensuring rules and regulations are followed. The dissemination of information and the cultivation of a collective commitment to responsible park visitation can be effectively accomplished through workshops, outreach programs, and social media campaigns.

In conclusion, being aware of and adhering to the laws and regulations of the park is an essential component of responsible outdoor activity. Parks are natural and cultural assets of great value, and they require careful management to ensure that they are preserved for future generations. Rules have been established to protect the environment, foster a sense of safety, and ensure that all visitors have a great experience. By following these norms, individuals contribute to their well-being and the larger purpose of conservation and stewardship. By educating themselves, participating in community activities, and making a collective commitment to responsible behavior, visitors can play an active role in the preservation of the beauty and integrity of our parks. This will ensure that these valued areas will continue for future generations.

Reservations and permits

Reservations and permits are essential in outdoor recreation because they offer a systematic framework for managing access to natural and cultural riches. Visitors and park management alike must be thoroughly aware of the complexities of reservations and permits, regardless of whether they are interested in exploring national parks, camping in wilderness regions, or taking guided tours. This article dives into the significance of reservations and permits, analyzing their function in promoting sustainable tourism, managing tourist numbers, preserving sensitive ecosystems, and guaranteeing a positive and equal experience for all individuals.

National parks and protected areas, famous for their scenic beauty and ecological significance, are visited by millions yearly. The implementation of reservation systems in many parks is done to strike a compromise between preserving these delicate settings and the demand for public access. Visitors can acquire entrance on specific dates and times through the use of reservations, which helps to manage crowd numbers and reduce congestion, particularly in locations that have limited capacity or are highly sensitive to the influence of humans. By implementing this strategy, the park can reduce its impact on the environment while simultaneously providing guests with a more delightful experience.

A further obstacle that needs to be addressed by the reservation system is the difficulty caused by the popularity of particular locations during peak seasons. Locations in great demand, such as iconic views, popular trails, or campgrounds, may have high attendance rates, which can result in congestion, the degradation of natural assets, and strains on infrastructure. Through the implementation of reservations, parks can divide visitors more uniformly, alleviating the strain placed on particular regions and improving the overall quality of the experience that visitors have. This strategy is consistent with sustainable tourism, which seeks to balance the enjoyment of natural wonders and the preservation of these priceless environments over the long term.

Obtaining permits and making reservations for some activities within parks and other protected areas are typically necessary. Backcountry camping, rock climbing, guided tours, and scientific research are all examples of activities that can be regulated and managed through permits. These licenses are designed to ensure that certain activities are carried out responsibly, thereby limiting their impact on the environment and other visitors. A permission system for backcountry camping, for instance, may restrict the number of campers that can be present in a particular region. This would prevent the area from being overused and would safeguard delicate ecosystems.

In addition, permits play an essential role in preserving cultural and historical sites and locations within parks. Limits may be placed on access to historic ruins, archeological sites, or culturally significant locations in certain regions to prevent disturbances that could undermine the integrity of these regions. Park administration can monitor and limit the amount of visitors to these sensitive locations by demanding permits for access. This allows them to balance public participation and preserving the surrounding environment.

Reservations and permits are not only essential for the management of access, but they also contribute to the generation of cash that can be used for the upkeep and improvement of parks. In many parks, visitors must pay fees to enter the park, camp there, and participate in particular activities. These fees are then used to fund infrastructure development, conservation initiatives, and educational programs. It is essential for parks to get this financial support to ensure their continuous viability and to ensure that they can satisfy the requirements of visitors while also preserving the ecological welfare of the area.

Some tourists, particularly those who love to travel on the spur of the moment, may find the procedure of making reservations and obtaining permits to be a cause of frustration even though it is required. Those opposed to reservation systems claim that they restrict spontaneity and may reject individuals who cannot arrange their visits several weeks in advance. The trade-off, on the other hand, is essential to strike a balance between the expectations of all visitors and the long-term preservation objectives of the park. It is a challenging endeavor that involves careful consideration of the park's distinctive traits, visiting patterns, and conservation priorities to achieve this balance.

Education and awareness are additional opportunities gained through planning, which can be accomplished through reservations and permissions. When visitors participate in the reservation process, they can acquire knowledge of the unique laws and regulations that are in place within the park. By cultivating an understanding of the significance of preserving these natural and cultural wonders for future generations, this educational component helps visitors develop a sense of responsibility, allowing tourists to create a sense of duty. Visitors are encouraged to embrace environmentally responsible activities and contribute to the park's conservation aims through the reservation process, which serves as a doorway to environmental stewardship.

The reservation and permit systems have been changed in recent years due to technological improvements, which have made them more accessible and efficient simultaneously. Visitors can now book admittance, campsites, or guided tours from the convenience of their own homes, thanks to the proliferation of online reservation platforms now available at many parks. This not only makes the procedure more accessible for visitors but also gives park management vital information on the patterns of visits, which enables them to make decisions that are more informed and improves the way resources are distributed by providing them with this information.

Even though significant gains have been made, implementing reservations and permits has challenges. Users may experience irritation due to problems such as system faults, website crashes, or limited access during busy hours. The demand for well-known parks and locations can also result in highly competitive reservation systems, making it like winning a lottery to get a space in the park or destination of your choice. To address these difficulties, it is necessary to commit to ongoing development. The park administration should investigate ways to improve the efficiency and fairness of the reservation and permission processes.

At the reservation and permission landscape, community engagement is an essential component that must be considered. When it comes to the management of parks, local communities frequently play an indispensable role, and the viewpoints of these groups are critical in the process of formulating reservation regulations. The incorporation of local communities into the decision-making processes not only helps to establish a sense of collective responsibility but also guarantees that the advantages of tourism are dispersed relatively. Furthermore, the development of sustainable tourism practices that strike a balance between the economic benefits of tourism and the preservation of local ecosystems and cultural heritage can result from partnerships with communities located close to the tourism destination.

It is essential to have flexible reservation and permit systems to cater to visitors' various requirements. Several parks provide a combination of reservable and first-come, first-served alternatives to accommodate both guests who plan ahead and those who are more spontaneous. Attaining a balance between accessibility and conservation can be facilitated by implementing adaptive management measures, such as modifying reservation quotas by seasonal demand. Developing an equitable system, welcoming to all and adaptable to the ever-changing requirements of visitors and the environment is the objective of this endeavor.

Reservations and permits are vital tools for managing access to parks and protected areas, contributing to the sustainability of outdoor leisure. The concerns of overuse, environmental deterioration, and cultural site protection are addressed by these mechanisms, which ensure that all visitors have a positive and equal experience. It is possible to acknowledge their benefits in preserving the environment, ensuring safety, and generating cash, even though they may present some difficulties, such as a restricted capacity for spontaneity and technological glitches. Visitors actively contribute to preserving our natural and cultural treasures by understanding and respecting the reservation and permit processes. This helps to ensure that these locations will continue to be accessible and awe-inspiring for future generations.

Leave-no-trace principles

The ethical cornerstone of responsible outdoor recreation is the Leave-No-Trace philosophy, which instructs people on reducing their environmental impact and maintaining the wilderness regions' natural beauty. Adopting sustainable methods becomes increasingly important as more and more people turn to the outdoors for peace. By encouraging environmental stewardship and striking a careful balance between enjoying the natural world and protecting it for future generations,
Leave-No-Trace acts as a set of recommendations. The importance of Leave-No-Trace guidelines is examined in this essay, along with their background, the fundamental ideas that direct responsible outdoor conduct, the advantages of adopting them, and their role in ensuring a sustainable future for the earth.

The concept of Leave-No-Trace originated with growing public awareness of the harm of outdoor activities to the environment. The mid-1900s saw a rise in outdoor recreation and a rising awareness of the vulnerability of ecosystems, which brought about the recognition that human activity was hurting formerly unspoiled wilderness places. Outdoor lovers, conservationists, and educators were motivated to reduce this impact, so they started developing the concepts that would eventually be called Leave-No-Trace. The intention was to encourage people to enjoy nature properly, causing as little disturbance as possible, rather than to dissuade them from doing so.

Leave-No-Trace is based on seven fundamental principles, each addressing a different facet of outdoor behavior. "Plan and Prepare," the first Principle, highlights the importance of completing homework before going on an outdoor trip. This entails preparing for garbage disposal, learning about legislation, and acquiring the required permissions. Sufficient planning reduces the probability of encountering unforeseen difficulties, resulting in a more seamless and responsible experience.

"Travel and Camp on Durable Surfaces," the second Principle, emphasizes how human traffic affects delicate ecosystems. It is advised that guests stick to designated routes and campsites to reduce this damage. By avoiding the construction of new paths, erosion, and habitat disruption are prevented, aiding in preserving the natural landscape. The ecosystem's integrity is maintained when use is limited to sturdy surfaces, guaranteeing that future generations can enjoy the same pristine beauty.

The third Principle: "Dispose of Waste Properly," highlights the importance of appropriate waste management. This entails removing all waste, litter, food scraps, and other biodegradable materials. In addition to preventing pollution and hazardous material ingestion by wildlife, proper disposal preserves the aesthetic value of natural areas. Adopting a "pack it in, pack it out" approach in locations lacking garbage disposal services is imperative.

The fourth rule, "Leave What You Find," advises tourists to respect cultural and ecological landmarks. An area's cultural history is undermined, and ecosystems' delicate equilibrium is upset when plants, rocks, or historical relics are disturbed. By observing these components without interfering with them, tourists aid in conserving the environment's inherent worth and historical importance.

The fifth Principle, "Minimize Campfire Impact," acknowledges the possible damage that campfires can cause to ecosystems. Visitors are recommended to utilize designated fire rings, keep fires small, and use only small sticks and twigs found on the ground while lighting fires. Ensuring all fires are out before departing guarantees that the most minor damage is done to the environment. It is advised to use portable stoves or other alternative cooking methods in regions where it is forbidden to start fires.

The sixth Principle, "Respect Wildlife," highlights the significance of keeping a safe and considerate distance from animals when observing them. Feeding wildlife can hurt their health by changing their natural habits and nutrition. Stress and endangerment can result from activities that disturb natural behaviors, such as trespassing on nesting grounds. Respecting wildlife keeps ecosystems intact and permits unhindered biological processes to occur.

The last rule, "Be Considerate of Other Visitors," emphasizes how outdoor areas are communal. An enjoyable and peaceful outdoor experience is enhanced by considering noise levels, sharing the route with others, and honoring other visitors' privacy. Being considerate of others guarantees no excessive disruptions to anyone's enjoyment of the outdoors and promotes a sense of shared responsibility.

Adopting the Leave-No-Trace guidelines has several short- and long-term advantages. Preserving the natural beauty of the surroundings is the most apparent benefit. These guidelines lessen the impact of humans on ecosystems, keeping them so they can flourish in their natural state. By preserving the environment, we can guarantee that future generations will be able to enjoy the same magnificent vistas and form a profound, pristine connection with nature.

Additionally, Leave-No-Trace is essential to conservation efforts. Endangered species and delicate habitats can be found in many natural regions. The principles buffer against accidental damage, preserve biodiversity, and advance general conservation objectives. Visitors actively contribute to protecting these delicate ecosystems by minimizing disturbances, sticking to approved pathways, and showing respect for wildlife. Another essential advantage of Leave-No-Trace guidelines is sustainable recreation. Adopting sustainable methods becomes crucial to preventing misuse and damage to natural environments as outdoor activities continue to gain popularity. Adhering to the guidelines reduces the impact on visitors, and the wear and tear on well-traveled paths and campgrounds is decreased. Using a sustainable approach, we can ensure that outdoor recreation is a rewarding and viable activity for future generations.
The tenets of Leave No Trace also support ecosystem resilience and general wellness. Outdoor enthusiasts contribute to preserving an area's ecological balance by abstaining from constructing new trails or campsites and

honoring its natural features. The natural world and human societies profit from the vital services that healthy ecosystems provide, such as pollination, clean water, and carbon sequestration.

Two essential elements of the Leave-No-Trace philosophy are awareness and education. The tenets form the basis for instructing outdoor enthusiasts on appropriate conduct in natural areas. Visitors are encouraged to practice environmental stewardship through outreach initiatives, interpretative signage, and educational resources that aid in disseminating these ideas. Leave-No-Trace fosters a community of conscientious outdoor enthusiasts who actively participate in environmental protection by raising awareness.

The Leave-No-Trace movement has been more popular worldwide in recent years. These ideas are incorporated into the policy and outreach initiatives of state and national parks, outdoor organizations, and educational institutions. The tenets have evolved into a symbol of acceptable outdoor ethics, influencing personal conduct, outdoor space management, and policy. This widespread adoption is indicative of a growing movement toward outdoor activity that is ethical and sustainable.

Even though the Leave-No-Trace guidelines provide a thorough manual for appropriate outdoor conduct, difficulties exist. It will take constant work to balance the growing demand for outdoor activities and the necessity of conservation. Visitor education, community involvement, and adaptive management techniques are essential to solve these issues. Finding a balance that permits people to enjoy nature while maintaining its purity is a dynamic process that necessitates cooperation and dedication from all parties involved—individuals, groups, and legislators.

In conclusion, the Leave-No-Trace philosophy demonstrates outdoor enthusiasts' dedication to protecting nature's treasures. These ethical principles serve as a road map for appropriate outdoor conduct, encouraging sustainability, conservation, and a closer relationship with the natural environment

CHAPTER IV

Planning Your Route

Researching National Park options

Individuals and families who are interested in engaging in meaningful outdoor activities should put in the effort to investigate the various National Park possibilities available to them. Because several national parks are located worldwide, each of which features distinctive topographies, a diverse range of flora and fauna, and chances for recreation, the process of picking the appropriate destination takes careful deliberation and extensive research. This paper investigates the value of researching the various National Park possibilities available, focusing on essential aspects such as geographical location, ecosystems, activities, accessibility, park laws, and visitor reviews. Prospective visitors can make educated judgments that align with their interests, preferences, and the kind of experience they are looking for when they have a thorough grasp of the various national parks and the unique services each provides.

While examining the many National Park alternatives,

the geographical location functions as a core factor. The expansive network of national parks encompasses a wide range of countries, continents, and ecological conditions. Some parks are located in coastal regions, enabling access to harsh shorelines and marine ecosystems, while others are set among towering mountain ranges, affording pristine alpine landscapes and spectacular panoramas. Both types of parks are located in the United States. In addition to impacting the park's climate, the park's geographical location also affects the kinds of flora and wildlife that can flourish there. Before delving into the specifics of the park, prospective tourists should consider their preferences regarding the climate, the topography, and the kinds of outdoor activities they enjoy doing.

It is essential for anyone who wishes to interact with nature and experience a variety of landscapes to have a solid understanding of the ecosystems that are contained inside a national park. Various ecosystems may be found inside each park, ranging from moist woods and dry deserts to alpine tundra and dense forests. Through the process of researching the ecosystems, visitors can gain an understanding of the ecological value of the park as well as predict the flora and wildlife that they may come across. The overall appreciation of a park's natural wonders is enhanced by having a comprehensive understanding of the park's ecosystems. This is true whether one is fascinated by the park's diverse plant life, the patterns of migratory birds, or the opportunity to come across elusive wildlife.

Within a national park, the activities and recreational possibilities that are accessible to visitors play a significant part in determining the overall experience that they have. The activities that may be found in parks cover a wide range of interests, from hiking and camping to wildlife observation, birdwatching, rock climbing, and water-based adventures. Parks are designed to accommodate a diverse range of interests. By researching the offered activities, visitors can ensure that their preferences and ability levels are compatible with the activities provided by the park. When visitors have a full grasp of the available activities, they can adapt their experiences to match the amount of adventure they prefer. This is true whether they are looking for challenging backcountry treks, serene lakeside camping, or possibilities for bird photography.

One of the practical considerations that comes into play when determining whether or not it is possible to visit a specific National Park is accessibility. Certain parks may be easily accessible by automobile, with well-maintained roads and developed infrastructure. On the other hand, other parks may require more brutal forms of transportation, such as trekking, boats, or even tiny aircraft. A park's closeness to the traveler's location, the many modes of transportation available, and the amount of time and effort required to reach the destination of choice are all important considerations for travelers. It is helpful to understand the accessibility of a park since it allows one to manage one's expectations better and ensures that the entire enjoyment of the visit is not sacrificed due to practical concerns.

The regulations and rules of the park are crucial components of the research process because they govern the behavior of visitors and maintain the integrity of the natural and cultural resources. There is a possibility that different parks will have various regulations about camping permits, access to the wilderness, policies for pets, and seasonal limits. To visit parks responsibly, conducting informational research and becoming acquainted with these restrictions is essential. Visitors contribute to the preservation of the environment and develop a pleasant and respectful relationship with the natural wonders and other park-goers by gaining knowledge of the park laws and adhering to them.

Visitors' reviews and first-hand reports are crucial in influencing the perspective of the various possibilities available at National Parks in this age of digital technology. Much knowledge can be obtained from those who have personally visited a particular park due to online platforms, travel forums, and social media availability. It is possible to gain insights into the real-life experiences of other visitors by reading reviews and personal tales. These experiences show the great qualities of a park and the potential obstacles that may be encountered there. Although individuals may have different preferences, the reviews presented here offer insightful viewpoints that can assist prospective travelers in making well-informed selections and gaining a better understanding of what to anticipate during their journey.

When researching the many National Park alternatives, it is also essential to investigate each attraction's cultural and historical components. The rich histories, historic cultural sites, and Indigenous heritage found in many parks are located there. The visitor's experience is enhanced when they better understand the artistic value of a garden, which fosters a closer connection with the land and the people who live there. Furthermore, parks frequently include interpretive programs, ranger-led talks, and educational materials that offer insights into the cultural and historical context of the area in which the park is located. By incorporating these components into the research process, visitors can comprehend the holistic value of a National Park that extends beyond the natural beauty of the destination.

Planning the itinerary and determining the most essential areas of interest within the park are equally vital aspects of the research process. The selection of the National Park itself is simply one component of the research process. To guarantee that visitors make the most of their time and experience the most critical aspects of the park, it is essential to research the most popular trails, vistas, and landmarks. They are gaining an understanding of the duration that is advised for particular activities, whether a day hike or a multi-day backpacking trip, which enables one to manage one's time effectively and can provide a more satisfying adventure.

Environmental concerns and conservation activities should also be a part of the study focus within a national park context. It is common for parks to participate in programs that aim to protect endangered species, preserve ecosystems, and reduce humans' negative influence on the environment. Those committed to appropriate outdoor ethics should show their support and admiration for these conservation activities. Volunteering options, financial contributions, and participation in educational programs are ways visitors can actively contribute to conserving the park's ecological integrity.

Researching the various National Park possibilities

entails more than just choosing a location; it is a dynamic and comprehensive process that requires individuals to connect their tastes, expectations, and beliefs with the products and services offered by each park. Prospective tourists acquire a thorough awareness of what each destination has to offer as they explore the range of landscapes, ecosystems, and recreational possibilities available in the many parks they are considering visiting. This well-informed strategy guarantees that the selected National Park satisfies and goes beyond the expectations of individuals looking to establish meaningful connections with nature, engage in exciting adventures, and contribute to preserving the most cherished landscapes in our world.

Creating an itinerary for a seamless journey

Creating an itinerary is the first step in guaranteeing a smooth and pleasurable trip. An itinerary, whether for a road trip, outdoor excursion, or vacation, guides passengers through a well-thought-out order of events and locations. This section examines the importance of planning an itinerary, going over essential factors, including travel goals, time management, researching the place, adaptability, and incorporating various activities. Travelers may maximize their experiences, make the most of their time, and reduce potential stress during their trip by knowing the components of a successful schedule.

Determining the trip's goals should be the first and foremost priority while planning an itinerary. Well- defined goals set the tone for the entire itinerary, regardless of the purpose—exploration, adventure, relaxation, or a mix. While leisure and rejuvenation may be the main priorities of a beach vacation, cultural exploration may place a higher priority on trips to historical sites, museums, and local monuments. Finding the journey's main goal gives you a foundation for choosing locations, things to do, and places to stay that support these goals.

A crucial component of designing an agenda is time management, which guarantees that visitors maximize their available time without feeling pressured or overburdened. Finding a balance between exploration and leisure can be achieved by estimating the vacation length and dividing the time between different activities. A realistic and doable timetable is made possible by considering the time needed for sightseeing, transport between locations, and any potential delays. Although it may be tempting to jam as much as possible into the schedule, leaving time for relaxation and flexibility helps you avoid burnout and makes room for unplanned adventures.

A well-informed itinerary must be created after conducting extensive destination research. Every place has its unique features, regional traditions, and practical issues. A thorough understanding of the local weather, cultural activities, and special needs—like reservations or entry permits—ensures visitors are ready for anything. Travel guides, internet sites, and suggestions from other tourists can offer insightful information about must-see attractions, undiscovered treasures, and authentic local experiences that might enhance the agenda.

A fundamental element of itinerary planning is flexibility, which enables travelers to adjust to unforeseen events or possibilities. A well-planned itinerary offers direction, but allowing for flexibility improves the whole trip experience. Be it exploring a quaint local market, spending more time at a picturesque viewpoint, or embarking on an unexpected culinary excursion, being flexible encourages discovery and serendipity. An agenda that balances between having a set schedule and being flexible can accommodate prearranged activities and unanticipated surprises.

When planning a trip, the transportation logistics must be considered. This includes figuring out which forms of transportation—flights, rental cars, public transportation, or a mix of these—are the most efficient. Time spent in transit is reduced, and time at the destination is increased when transportation schedules are synchronized with scheduled activities. Furthermore, accounting for possible delays, traffic jams, or weather variations guarantees that the itinerary is flexible enough to accommodate last-minute alterations.

A vital component of the trip's overall success is the accommodations. They are researching and reserving lodging in advance, which is convenient and safer, especially during the busiest travel times. The decision-making process considers various factors, including facilities, reviews from prior visitors, and the distance from important sites. In addition to providing a foundation for rest, lodgings are carefully chosen to maximize itinerary efficiency and let visitors spend as much time as possible at each location.

Including various activities gives the schedule depth and richness while accommodating a range of interests and preferences. A well-rounded journey is achieved by balancing leisure periods, gastronomic excursions, outdoor adventures, and cultural experiences. Traveling with activities complementing the destination's special offers guarantees a more genuine and immersive experience. Whether going to a local festival, taking a picturesque trek, or sampling the area's cuisine, incorporating a variety of activities results in a comprehensive and unforgettable schedule.

Downtime is a factor that is frequently disregarded when creating itineraries. Though there's no denying the thrill of seeing new places, a well-balanced trip must include downtime for contemplation and relaxation. Visitors can relax and appreciate a destination's subtleties through various activities such as spending a peaceful afternoon at a café, meandering through a picturesque town square, or simply taking in the atmosphere. Including deliberate quiet times makes the journey more enjoyable and sustainable.

One pragmatic factor that improves the itinerary's efficiency is seamless communication. Keeping in touch via local SIM cards, messaging apps, and smartphone apps with other travelers, tour guides, and lodging providers guarantees that everyone is in the know. Effective communication makes coordination easier, gives real-time updates, and takes care of any unanticipated problems that might come up while traveling. Using technology to arrange the itinerary improves connectivity and convenience for the duration of the trip.

A practical and sustainable itinerary must consider the journey's financial factors. Comprehending the charges linked to lodging, transportation, activities, food, and other incidentals enables tourists to establish a spending plan and arrive at well-informed judgments. By investigating less expensive options, such as public transportation or reasonably priced restaurants, tourists can maximize their budget without sacrificing the pleasure of their trip. A well-managed budget makes travel less stressful and permits more deliberate resource allocation.

Traveling is better when the itinerary is concluded thoughtfully. A positive and thoughtful attitude is fostered when the itinerary is viewed as a framework that adjusts to the flow of the voyage instead of a strict set of instructions. To connect with the trip experience more deeply, reflect on the day's events, welcome the unexpected, and cherish the happy and exciting times.

When this thoughtful approach is applied, the itinerary becomes a meaningful narrative of the journey instead of just a logistical plan.

In summary, planning an itinerary is a deliberate and purposeful procedure determining how a voyage unfolds. Through the alignment of travel goals, efficient time management, comprehensive destination research, adoption of flexibility, and thoughtful consideration of pragmatic factors, tourists can design an itinerary that maximizes their experiences. A schedule that is well-planned streamlines travel logistics, incorporates a variety of activities, and provides downtime. A pleasant trip is guaranteed by seamless communication with other passengers and service providers, and a joyful and sustainable experience is enhanced by careful budgetary planning. In the end, a well-planned itinerary is an invaluable resource that helps visitors navigate the places they have selected and turns the trip into a rich tapestry of exploration, learning, and unique experiences.

Tips for on-the-road navigation and route adjustments

Proficiency in on-the-road navigation and route modifications is essential for travelers starting road excursions or undertaking adventures when adaptability is necessary. Road trips sometimes include navigating foreign territory, facing unforeseen hurdles, and adjusting to shifting conditions. This post examines helpful advice for efficient route modifications and on- the-road navigation, emphasizing technology, readiness, situational awareness, alternate routes, and the significance of welcoming the unexpected. Travelers may improve their road trip experiences, make wise judgments, and turn unforeseen obstacles into chances for exploration by developing these abilities.

In the present day, embracing technology is essential to efficient on-road navigation. Due to the widespread use of smartphones and navigation apps, visitors can access many valuable resources. Real-time information about routes, traffic, and possible road closures can be obtained using GPS apps like Google Maps, Waze, or specialized navigation systems. These apps provide turn-by-turn directions, alternate routes, and projected arrival times, enabling drivers to make wise decisions while driving. Maintaining an internet connection also allows real-time modifications based on traffic updates, making the trip more efficient and seamless.

Even with the increasing reliance on technology, travelers must have backup navigational strategies ready. GPS signals can be weakened in isolated locations or during unforeseen technical malfunctions. As a backup, carrying paper maps, atlases, or a non-cellular navigation device provides a dependable way to navigate if digital options aren't available. A well-prepared traveler can make their way around with assurance, even in the face of potential technological difficulties.

To navigate while driving, one must maintain situational awareness, which calls for constant vigilance and observation of one's surroundings. Verifying the accuracy of navigational directions is made more accessible by keeping an eye out for mile markers, road signs, and landmarks. Travelers should proactively anticipate obstacles and make educated decisions by being aware of local traffic patterns, weather, and probable detours. Beyond merely using technology, situational awareness entails actively interacting with the surroundings and remaining aware of the subtleties of the trip.

An essential component of efficient on-the-road navigation is pre-trip planning. Before leaving, travelers should prepare and investigate their itinerary, noting important destinations, waypoints, and probable obstacles. Proactive route changes are made possible by thoroughly understanding the geography, road conditions, and potential construction zones. Planning also entails considering rest areas, places to eat, and places to stay the night, guaranteeing a relaxing and well-rounded trip. Travelers are better prepared to drive confidently and efficiently when they have done extensive pre-trip planning.

It is a virtue to be flexible when navigating when driving. Even with careful preparation, unanticipated events like construction, road closures, or unplanned detours can cause the original route to be disrupted. When travelers adopt a flexible mindset and stop considering these obstacles as obstacles, they can change course and look for other options. The flexibility to modify the schedule in response to current events encourages resilience and adaptability. This adaptability turns unforeseen difficulties into chances for lucky finds and thrilling excursions.

An essential quality of seasoned travelers is their capacity to adapt their plans in light of evolving conditions. Dynamic elements such as traffic patterns, road closures, and weather-related difficulties may require last-minute alterations. Keeping in touch with fellow travelers, radio traffic updates, and navigation apps can help you stay informed about the state of the roads. Making quick decisions when necessary is possible by having a backup plan and thinking through alternate pathways beforehand. The secret is approaching route changes with a level head and seeing them as opportunities for adventure rather than roadblocks.

Local expertise and community insights are essential resources for on-the-road navigation. Gaining insight into the road conditions and potential difficulties can be facilitated by interacting with locals, making recommendations, and consulting other tourists for information. Locals frequently know detours, picturesque side streets, and hidden treasures that are not readily visible with conventional navigational aids. Building relationships with the locals enhances the travel experience with genuine advice and firsthand insights and promotes a sense of solidarity.

Maintaining a car regularly is an important but sometimes disregarded part of road navigation. A well-kept vehicle lessens the chance of unplanned problems or breakdowns when traveling. Pre-trip vehicle tests ensure that the car is roadworthy, which include tire pressure, fluid levels, brakes, and general mechanical condition. In the event of unforeseen mechanical problems, having a roadside help kit, a spare tire, and necessary tools offers security. A smooth travel experience starts with a dependable car, which frees travelers from unwarranted worries about vehicle dependability so they can concentrate on navigation and route modifications.

It takes a thorough grasp of the difficulties presented by various settings to navigate through multiple terrains and weather situations. Coastal locales may have problems with exposure to saltwater and extreme humidity, while mountainous regions may have steep inclines, winding roads, and other altitude-related challenges. Educating oneself on the unique obstacles linked to the intended path improves one's capacity for efficient navigation and well-informed route modifications. Customizing navigation tactics to each environment's distinct features guarantees a

Effective time management plays a crucial role in road navigation, impacting choices about rest stops, overnight stays, and the general pace of the trip. An optimum travel experience includes knowing how long the journey is expected, accounting for rest stops, and scheduling breaks at fascinating locations or picturesque vistas. Flexibility in the itinerary is another benefit of effective time management, as it enables impromptu stops or extended stays at charming locations. A satisfying road trip involves balancing moving forward with the adventure and setting aside time for exploration.

For the travel party to navigate the road together, communication is crucial. Everyone will agree if clear communication channels are established, whether via cell phones, walkie-talkies, or in-car communication systems. Talking about rest stops, route modifications, and possible itinerary alterations promotes a cooperative and well-organized travel experience. Good communication reduces miscommunication, increases security, and fosters a sense of shared accountability among passengers.

The experience of on-the-road navigation is enhanced by adopting an attitude of acceptance for the unexpected. Even with careful planning, road vacations are bound to include unexpected pleasures and surprises. Divergences from the itinerary, impromptu events, and chance meetings enhance the journey's complexity. Travelers can relish the fate of the road when they embrace the unexpected rather than seeing departures from the original plan as interruptions. These spontaneous encounters frequently become the most memorable parts of the journey, leaving enduring memories and exciting tales to tell.

In summary, navigating while driving and modifying a route necessitates a comprehensive strategy that integrates technology, readiness, adaptability, and an optimistic outlook. Travelers can navigate more skillfully by using navigation apps, being organized with backup plans, and keeping situational awareness. Embracing flexibility makes it possible to adapt to changing circumstances, and local expertise and community insights improve the overall navigation experience. An easy ride is facilitated by routine car maintenance, knowledge of various terrains, and efficient time management. Coordination within the trip group is ensured by communication, and possibilities for exploration are created when obstacles are met with open arms. Gaining proficiency in these areas improves the usefulness of on-the-road navigation and the whole road trip experience, making it a vibrant and unforgettable journey.

CHAPTER V

Campground Etiquette

Proper campground behavior

An enjoyable and peaceful camping experience depends on campers behaving appropriately, guaranteeing they get along with the environment, other campers, and nature. The number of people finding comfort in nature is growing, which makes appropriate camping practices even more crucial. The importance of proper campground behavior is examined in this essay, which also examines essential ideas, including respect for other campers, noise control, waste disposal, campfire etiquette, and Leave-No-Trace ethics. Campers help to preserve the natural beauty of the outdoors, maintain the health of ecosystems, and build a happy and sustainable outdoor community by being aware of and abiding by these values.

Go-No-WhereThe foundation of appropriate camping behavior is trace ethics, which emphasize the significance of reducing environmental effects and maintaining the integrity of natural areas. The guiding principles support careful planning, appropriate disposal of waste, and a dedication to preserving the integrity of ecosystems. Starting with the idea of "Plan Ahead and Prepare," campers are urged to learn about the particular rules of the campground, secure the required permits, and pack appropriately. Sufficient planning reduces the possibility of unanticipated difficulties and enhances the overall camping experience.

The book "Travel and Camp on Durable Surfaces" emphasizes how human activity affects delicate ecosystems. Adhering to designated pathways and campgrounds can prevent unnecessarily trampling plants, erosion, and ecosystem disturbance. Conscientious campers understand the importance of protecting the surrounding environment, staying on approved routes, and leaving as little imprint as possible. This idea makes sure that the campground's beauty will be preserved for enjoyment by future generations.

The first rule of appropriate camping etiquette is to

"Dispose of Waste Properly." Campers are expected to remove all rubbish, even biodegradable items like food scraps, to avoid pollution and save animals. The "pack it in, pack it out" philosophy strongly emphasizes individual accountability for waste disposal. Campers must take out all trash and leave the campground in the same condition as when they arrived in locations without specified waste disposal facilities. Maintaining campground cleanliness and ecological health depends on responsible garbage disposal.

The motto "Leave What You Find" invites campers to

respect and value cultural and natural assets without interfering with them. Disturbing historical relics, plants, or rocks can have a lasting effect on cultural heritage and ecosystems. Conscientious campers recognize the need to maintain the campground's natural beauty and historical relevance by leaving these components unaltered. This idea encourages a conservationist mindset and a dedication to preserving the outdoor spaces' cultural and biological integrity.

The article "Minimize Campfire Impact" discusses the

possible damage campfires can do to the environment. It is recommended that campers only use small sticks and twigs that are found on the ground, keep fires modest, and use designated fire rings. Ensuring all fires are out before departing guarantees that the most minor damage is done to the environment. Campers should utilize portable stoves or other alternate cooking methods in places where fires are prohibited. Maintaining air quality, averting wildfires, and protecting the environment depends on proper campfire etiquette.

"Respect Wildlife" highlights the importance of keeping a safe and respectful distance when observing wildlife. Feeding wildlife or trying to get up close and personal with them might upset their natural routine and lead to dangerous dependency. Conscientious campers recognize the value of wildlife in their natural environment and refrain from actions that could cause them harm or disturbance. Campers contribute to ecosystems' general well-being and equilibrium by showing respect for wildlife.

The phrase "Be Considerate of Other Visitors" emphasizes how public outdoor areas are. Conscientious campers consider their noise levels, give way to others on the route, and honor other guests' privacy. Being considerate of others makes camping enjoyable and peaceful, allowing everyone to enjoy the outdoors without excessive disruptions. This idea fosters a community-focused mindset and a sense of shared responsibility in campers.

A vital component of appropriate campground etiquette is noise management, which extends beyond the Leave-No-Trace maxim of showing consideration for fellow campers. People go to campgrounds to find peace and connect to the natural world. An overabundance of noise can ruin the tranquil atmosphere and make camping less enjoyable for other people. Conscientious campers minimize noise disturbance by using headphones, keeping to quiet hours, and participating in activities that limit loud noises. This method encourages a courteous and welcoming environment, enabling campers to live in harmony with one another.

Requirements for disposing of waste go beyond the Leave-No-Trace policy and are an essential component of responsible campground conduct. Campers are required to manage their waste carefully, including properly disposing of human waste and packing out rubbish. When camping in places without designated restrooms, campers should dig catholes 200 feet away from water sources and at least six to eight inches deep, adhering to the Leave-No-Trace principle. Other possibilities include bringing a portable toilet or using it if camping amenities are available. In addition to keeping the campground hygienic, proper trash disposal keeps water sources from contamination.

Campfire etiquette is a fundamental component of appropriate camping conduct, which is closely linked to the Leave-No-Trace guidelines. Responsible campers follow the campground rules and use the allotted fire rings when it comes to fires. They avoid disturbing living plants by gathering only tiny, dead wood they find on the ground for their fire. Campers ensure their fires are completely extinguished before departing, keeping them small and controlled. Cooking appliances or portable stoves are used in places where it is forbidden to start fires. Adherence to campfire restrictions is essential to keep the campground safe, avoid wildfires, and safeguard the ecosystem.

The Leave-No-Trace guidelines and consideration for other campers go hand in hand, highlighting the significance of fostering a welcoming and positive camping environment. Conscientious campers refrain from actions that could annoy other campgrounds, showing consideration for others' personal space and privacy. This entails utilizing low-impact lighting, avoiding invasive behaviors, and minimizing noise during specified quiet hours. A good camping experience is enhanced for everyone by campers who cultivate a sense of community and shared responsibility.

An essential component of appropriate campground etiquette is responsible pet ownership. Pets are welcome at many campgrounds, but campers must follow specific rules and regulations. This entails picking up after pets, keeping them on leashes, and ensuring they don't bother other campers or wildlife. Responsible pet owners also think about their pets' comfort and safety, giving them access to enough water, shelter, and protection from foul weather. Campers positively impact the peaceful and pleasurable camping experience by adhering to pet-related restrictions and exercising proper pet ownership.

Outreach programs and educational campaigns are essential for encouraging appropriate camping behavior. Campgrounds, park officials, and outdoor organizations can work together to educate campers on Leave-No-Trace guidelines, campground policies, and appropriate outdoor activities. Ranger-led presentations, internet materials, interpretive programs, and signs can all help achieve this. These organizations enable campers to make wise decisions and take responsible actions while enjoying their camping experiences by bringing awareness to the issue and offering educational resources.

Participation in the community and stewardship programs supports the group's goal of encouraging appropriate campground conduct. Campers can get involved in planned cleanup days, trail upkeep initiatives, and environmental preservation campaigns. Through these programs, outdoor enthusiasts are encouraged to feel a sense of belonging and shared responsibility for the upkeep of campgrounds and natural areas. Campers can actively contribute to the sustainability and preservation of the outdoor settings they value by participating in stewardship activities.

In summary, ethical outdoor enjoyment necessitates appropriate camping behavior to protect the environment's natural beauty and the health of ecological systems. The cornerstone of ethical camping is Leave-No-Trace ethics, which emphasizes values including careful planning, disposal of garbage, and reducing environmental effects. It is recommended that campers moderate noise levels, show consideration for other guests, and follow campsite policies regulating pets and campfires. Responsible campsite behavior is a group effort to build a welcoming, inclusive, and sustainable outdoor community. It extends beyond individual acts. By adhering to these values, campers promote a culture of respect, accountability, and appreciation for the great outdoors, thereby contributing to enjoying natural environments for present and future generations.

Respecting fellow campers and wildlife

Creating a harmonic balance between human enjoyment and preserving natural ecosystems is crucial to responsible outdoor recreation. One of the essential aspects of responsible outdoor recreation is respecting fellow campers and wildlife. It is becoming increasingly important to cultivate a peaceful coexistence with fellow campers and the various species of wildlife that inhabit these spaces as the number of people seeking shelter in the great outdoors continues to increase. This essay delves into multiple topics: noise management, campsite etiquette, responsible pet ownership, wildlife observation methods, and the broader implications of developing a healthy outdoor community. It examines the myriad of facets that comprise the concept of respecting fellow campers and animals.

One of the most critical aspects of respecting other campers is the ability to control one's level of loudness and show consideration for the need for others to have peace in the natural setting. Individuals looking for a place to escape the hustle and bustle of city life and immerse themselves in the sounds of nature often go to campgrounds. Campers who observe responsible camping practices are aware of the impact that excessive noise can have on the camping experience of others and stick to the recommended quiet hours. It is important to remember that talks should be kept at a moderate volume, that loud music and activities that could be disturbing should be avoided during these designated periods, and that headphones should be worn when personally enjoying entertainment. Campers contribute to a great camping experience for everyone by creating a calm and serene environment. This facilitates the ability of each individual to appreciate the tranquility found in the natural environment.

Campground etiquette is essential since it helps foster a sense of community and respect among campers, which is critical to the success of outdoor activities. Campers who are responsible are aware of their surroundings and take precautions to ensure that their actions do not violate the privacy or space of other campsites. To accomplish this, it is necessary to resist wandering into the designated areas of other campers, respect the limits that have been set, and maintain a level of decorum that demonstrates an appreciation of shared spaces. Campers should also be conscious of their use of communal amenities such as restrooms and water sources, and they should make sure that these resources are left in a clean and functional condition for other campers to use. Campers contribute to a good and thoughtful outdoor community by following campground etiquette, which fosters a shared sense of responsibility for the well-being of the place where they are camping. Responsibly owning a pet is another essential component of showing respect to other campers and ensuring the safety and well-being of animals. Even though many campgrounds allow campers to bring their pets, campers are expected to comply with specific laws to guarantee a pleasant experience for everyone.

Essential measures include keeping pets on leashes, cleaning up after them, and keeping them from disrupting other campers or wildlife. In addition, competent pet owners consider the comfort and safety of their animals by providing them with sufficient shelter, water, and protection from adverse weather conditions. Campers may establish an atmosphere where everyone can enjoy the outdoors without having to worry about interruptions or safety concerns related to animals by adhering to recommendations unique to pets.

In addition to showing consideration for other campers, one of the most important aspects of ethical outdoor leisure is respecting the present animals. Camping grounds and other natural areas are frequent destinations for people who want to feel more connected to the natural world and observe animals in their natural environment. The well-being of animals and the ecosystems in which they live is given the utmost importance in responsible wildlife observation methods. These techniques ensure that the presence of humans does not excessively disturb or harm wildlife. Campers need to keep a safe and respectful distance from wildlife. Instead of approaching animals directly, they should use binoculars or zoom lenses to get a closer look at them. To ensure the safety of campers and preserve the animals' natural habits, it is of the utmost importance to refrain from making unexpected movements, making loud noises, or attempting to feed or engage with wildlife under any circumstances.

Additionally, to show respect for wildlife, it is necessary to comprehend and adhere to the specific restrictions or guidelines that park authorities or wildlife management agencies have established. The purpose of these laws is to safeguard not only the animals but also the people who come to visit. Campers must be informed of any limitations that may apply to feeding wildlife, approaching specific species, or entering restricted areas. The responsible observation of wildlife not only helps to protect the safety of campers and the animals, but it also contributes to the overall ecological health of the geographical area. The commitment to preserving the wildness and natural behaviors of wildlife makes it possible for them to flourish in the environments in which they were initially found.

Additionally, ethical campers are aware of the potential influence their presence may have on the habitats and habits of wildlife around the area. One of the most important practices is to select campsites that cause the slightest disturbance to animal corridors and nesting locations. It is also important to follow established routes to prevent trampling delicate flora. Campers should avoid introducing non-native species, fire restrictions should be followed to prevent habitat loss, and waste should be disposed of appropriately to reduce the likelihood of encounters with wildlife. Campers become stewards of the natural environment when they understand the interconnection of the ecosystem. This allows them to actively contribute to the preservation of biodiversity and the overall health of the ecosystem.

Developing a community that can survive in the great outdoors requires a collective commitment to responsible behavior that goes beyond the activities of individual members. Campers are part of a larger community of people who enjoy being outside and have a common respect for the natural world and a strong desire to preserve its splendor. Participating in community projects and stewardship programs helps cultivate a sense of collective responsibility for keeping wild places and campgrounds. Through their participation in scheduled clean-up events, trail maintenance initiatives, and environmental conservation programs, campers have the opportunity to contribute actively to the preservation and sustainability of outdoor ecosystems. They can become a driving force for good change and environmental activism if they collaborate to address issues such as litter, habitat degradation, and invasive species.

When you show consideration for your fellow campers and the animals that live in the area, you are not only fulfilling an ethical obligation but also ensuring that future generations will continue to have access to and enjoy the benefits of outdoor places. The influence of human activities on natural ecosystems is becoming more noticeable as the number of people who participate in outdoor recreation activities increases. Appropriate camping practices, which include noise management, campground etiquette, proper pet ownership, and wildlife observation techniques, serve as a model for creating a sustainable and peaceful outdoor community. Through the adoption of these values, campers contribute to the conservation of natural beauty, the maintenance of ecosystems, and the development of a positive culture of the outdoors, one in which respect for both fellow campers and wildlife is of the utmost importance.

Leave-no-trace camping practices

The Leave No Trace camping practices are dedicated to responsible and sustainable outdoor recreation. These practices emphasize the significance of reducing the amount of influence that humans have on natural surroundings. Considering the growing number of people looking for peace and excitement in the great outdoors, adhering to responsible camping practices is becoming increasingly important. This essay delves into themes such as meticulous preparation, correct trash disposal, low-impact camping techniques, respect for wildlife, and the broader implications of cultivating a culture of environmental stewardship. The critical concepts of Leave-No-Trace camping are discussed in depth throughout this section.

When it comes to camping, the Leave No Trace philosophy places a strong emphasis on the importance of meticulous preparation. Campers who are responsible know that the first step in reducing their environmental impact is to take precautions before they ever enter the wilderness. For this purpose, careful planning is required, which includes researching the specific restrictions of the chosen camping place and adhering to those regulations, getting the requisite permissions, and gaining an awareness of the particular environmental factors peculiar to the region. Campers can reduce the likelihood of encountering potential difficulties and contribute to the conservation of the natural landscape they wish to explore if they arrive well-prepared.

The concept of Leave No Trace camping emphasizes the obligation of campers to pack out all garbage and leave the environment in the same pristine condition they found it in. Proper waste disposal is a cornerstone of this camping philosophy. Not only does this include more visible things like food wrappers, but it also includes biodegradable materials like food leftovers like meal wrappers. "Pack it in, pack it out" is a catchphrase that stresses the idea that if something was brought into the wilderness, it should also be carried out of the wilderness itself. Campers responsible for their actions bring robust trash bags to dispose of rubbish, guaranteeing that no leftovers are left behind.

Additionally, this commitment to disposing of all garbage includes waste disposal from human beings. Those who camp in locations that do not have permanent bathroom facilities are expected to adhere to the Leave-No-Trace requirements, which require them to dig catholes that are at least six to eight inches deep and are located at least 200 feet away from any water sources. To actively contribute to preserving the ecological integrity and cleanliness of the camping area, campers are responsible for precise trash management.

Campers are encouraged to tread lightly and decrease their environmental footprint using tactics that have minimal environmental influence. These approaches are at the basis of Leave-No-Trace principles. This entails camping in approved areas and along pathways that have already been developed to cause the least harm to the vegetation and wildlife. Responsible campers use long-lasting surfaces like rock, gravel, or established campsites when setting up their tents. This allows them to avoid damaging delicate ecosystems that are susceptible to damage. In addition, campers adhere to the philosophy of "Leave What You Find," which states that they should not pluck plants, disturb rocks, or engage in other activities that can potentially change the natural landscape. Campers actively contribute to preserving delicate areas and ensuring that the outdoor places will stay pristine for future generations by adopting these approaches that have a minimum impact on the environment.

The Leave No Trace camping philosophy considers the significance of preserving the natural behaviors and habitats of the various species that live in the wilderness. As a result, the concept of wildlife respect is an essential component of this philosophy. As a kind of ethical wildlife observation, campers keep a safe distance from the animals they observe and use binoculars or zoom lenses to have a closer look at them rather than approaching them directly. There is a strong prohibition against making loud noises, unexpected movements, and attempting to feed or engage with endangered animals. This commitment to courteously interacting with wildlife assures the safety of campers and the animals and contributes to the area's general ecological health. Campers become stewards of the natural environment and actively participate in the protection of biodiversity when they get a grasp of the interconnectivity of ecosystems by learning about it firsthand.

It is important to note that the Leave-No-Trace practices cover individual activities and broader implications for developing a culture that values environmental stewardship. One of the most critical roles that education plays in fostering awareness and comprehension of the concepts that underlie Leave-No-Trace camping is that of education. Campers, outdoor organizations, and park authorities can participate in educational activities through interpretive programs, internet resources, ranger-led talks, and interactive signage. Through these efforts, campers are given the ability to make decisions based on accurate information. They are encouraged to develop a sense of responsibility for the health of the natural ecosystems that they travel through.

In addition, the promotion of Leave-No-Trace camping practices is aided by the contribution of community participation and stewardship efforts to the overall endeavor. Campers can participate in scheduled activities such as trail maintenance projects, environmental conservation programs, and opportunities to clean up the environment. In addition to instilling a sense of shared responsibility for the maintenance and sustainability of the outside environments that outdoor lovers hold dear, these projects also promote a sense of community among those who like spending time outside. Campers become active contributors to the cleanliness, health, and long-term sustainability of natural habitats when participating in stewardship-related activities.

Leave No Trace camping is a set of principles that urge campers to make informed decisions based on the individual qualities of each camping place. These principles are not inflexible regulations but guidelines that can be adapted to suit particular circumstances. The Leave-No-Trace practices emphasize the significance of adapting camping activities following the needs of the environment, considering that different surroundings may have varied sensitivities. In arid places, for example, the influence of human presence on fragile desert ecosystems may be more pronounced, which is why it is necessary to pay increased attention to practices with less impact. On the other hand, campers in thickly forested areas may need to consider the heightened risk of wildfires and implement specific steps to prevent unintentional igniting. This versatility guarantees that the principles of Leave No Trace can be used everywhere while respecting each natural habitat's distinctive characteristics.

Regarding broader conversations about sustainable and environmentally friendly living, Leave No Trace camping practices overlap with such discussions. The principles of Leave-No-Trace provide a framework for extending responsible conduct to outdoor recreation, which is becoming increasingly important as people become more aware of their influence on the environment in all aspects of their lives. A worldwide trend toward sustainability aligns with the philosophy of limiting waste, decreasing ecological damage, and cultivating an understanding of the inherent worth of natural environments. Camping enthusiasts who adhere to the Leave No Trace philosophy contribute positively to the health of particular camping locations and align themselves with a more significant commitment to living in an environmentally conscientious manner.

Camping methods that adhere to the Leave No Trace principle are, in conclusion, a philosophy that promotes responsible and environmentally conscious outdoor leisure. Campers actively contribute to preserving natural beauty and ecological health by emphasizing the importance of comprehensive preparation, efficient waste disposal, techniques that have a minimal impact on the environment, and respectful observation of wildlife. Leave-No-Trace is a set of values that include not just the acts of individuals but also broader consequences, such as education, community engagement, and a dedication to environmental stewardship. In adopting these practices, campers cultivate a culture of responsibility, an appreciation for the natural environment, and a commitment to leaving no trace behind. As a result of their actions, individuals play a significant part in ensuring that future generations will have the opportunity to continue awestruck by the natural beauties that the world has to offer.

CHAPTER VI

Meals on the Road

Planning and preparing RV-friendly meals

Planning and preparing RV-friendly meals is pivotal to ensuring a seamless and enjoyable road trip experience. Cooking in a camper trailer presents particular difficulties and limitations that require careful planning and methodical preparation. This essay examines the essential components of organizing and cooking meals suitable for an RV. It covers meal preparation, small kitchen necessities, adaptable products, and inventive cooking methods. Travelers may enjoy tasty and nourishing meals while on the road, improve the entire experience, and maximize convenience by learning the art of RV-friendly meal preparation.

Planning meals effectively starts with carefully considering the tools and kitchen area available in an RV. Because RV kitchens are small, efficiency and usefulness must be prioritized. It's essential to assess the kitchen's amenities, including the stove's size, the refrigerator's capacity, and the amount of counter space available, before leaving on a road trip. Equipped with this understanding, vacationers can arrange meals that complement what their RV kitchen can provide. Meal preparation becomes a valuable tactic since it makes organizing ingredients possible and speeds up cooking when traveling.

The secret to successful meal preparation for an RV is choosing adaptable items. Selecting products that work well in several dishes cuts down on the amount of ingredients you need to carry and increases the range of meals you may make. Different recipes can be built around staples such as rice, pasta, canned beans, and various seasonings. Carrots, bell peppers, and onions are examples of fresh produce that have a longer shelf life and add taste and nutrition to meals without needing to be refrigerated constantly. Travelers can minimize the need for a large pantry by carefully selecting adaptable and delicious items.

Essentials for a small kitchen are critical to the effectiveness of meal preparation in an RV. Purchasing collapsible utensils, space-saving cookware, and multipurpose kitchen appliances maximizes an RV's little counter and storage area. A toaster oven, electric skillet, or slow cooker are portable gadgets that can increase cooking possibilities without taking up too much space. Travelers may make the most of their roadside cooking adventures by making the most out of every kitchen tool. Thanks to the thoughtful selection of small kitchen necessities, every square inch of the RV kitchen is efficiently used.

RV-friendly meal planning emphasizes meal prep as a crucial tactic that helps travelers cut down on time and streamline cooking while on the road. People can chop vegetables, marinate proteins, and prepare and portion things before heading on the road. These prepared ingredients are ready for quick and easy meal assembly; they can be kept in small containers or resealable bags. Preparing meals ahead of time expedites the cooking process and reduces the amount of work that must be done in the tiny kitchen of an RV. Travelers who set aside time to prepare their meals in advance can benefit from the easy and stress-free cooking that comes with traveling.

Meals fit for an RV can be made even more exciting and versatile using creative cooking techniques. For example, grilling enables visitors to enjoy the taste of outdoor cooking while utilizing small, lightweight grills that are appropriate for use with recreational vehicles.

Recipes for one pot or pan make cleanup more accessible by reducing the number of dishes and cookware you need to manage in your small kitchen. The ease of cooking in an RV is further enhanced by embracing the convenience of foil packet meals, in which components are wrapped in foil and cooked simultaneously. These inventive methods address the logistics of living in an RV while enhancing the cooking experience.

Flexibility is a valuable mentality when organizing and preparing meals suitable for an RV. Meal preparation must be flexible due to various factors, including the availability of fresh produce, accessibility to grocery stores, and the possibility of unforeseen changes in the travel schedule. Making a flexible meal plan enables you to make changes in response to unexpected culinary ideas, changes in the availability of ingredients, and local culinary influences. By embracing flexibility, tourists may make the most of their roadside gastronomic explorations and transform obstacles into chances for inventive cooking.

Meal planning for an RV must start with efficient storage techniques because there is little room in the refrigerator or pantry. Making the most of the available space when keeping supplies, leftovers, and processed components is accomplished using stackable and small containers. Preserving perishable goods for extended periods can be achieved using vacuum-sealed bags or airtight containers. Keeping the refrigerator, cupboards, and drawers in the RV kitchen organized makes it easier to get items and reduces the possibility of spills or spoiling while traveling. Effective storage techniques help keep a kitchen tidy and make it easier for guests to move about their cooking area.

Adopting the ease of premade and packaged goods can be a sensible strategy for meal preparation suitable for an RV. Cooking can be significantly streamlined using products like pre-cut veggies, canned soups, or pre-cooked proteins, as long as freshness and convenience are balanced. When cooking in the small space of an RV kitchen, these practical choices are time-saving alternatives. When premium pre-packaged foods are chosen, travelers can have filling, tasty meals without sacrificing flavor or nutrients.

RV-friendly meal planning considers environmental factors like waste minimization and sustainable options. Choosing reusable bags, cutlery, and environmentally friendly cooking supplies is consistent with a desire to reduce the environmental effect of travel. In addition, tourists should favor seasonal and locally sourced foods, lowering the carbon footprint of long-distance food transportation and promoting regional agriculture. Making thoughtful meal preparation decisions helps make RV travel more ecologically friendly and sustainable.

RV-friendly meal planning gains a wonderful dimension from the discovery of regional cuisine. Explore specialized shops, local grocery stores, and farmers' markets to learn about regional flavors and distinctive ingredients. A meal's cultural diversity can be enhanced using regional specialty foods, spices, or fruit. Accepting the variety of regional food makes meals more enjoyable and helps visitors get a taste of each place they visit.

Culinary creativity and experimentation are encouraged when creating and cooking meals that are suitable for an RV. A dynamic and pleasurable culinary experience can be made by experimenting with new recipes, modifying well-known meals to fit the limitations of the RV kitchen, and learning new cooking techniques. Every meal provides an opportunity to investigate the possibilities within the confines of RV living, turning the trip into a gourmet adventure. Travelers may make meal preparation an enjoyable and fulfilling part of their road trip experiences by encouraging a creative spirit in the kitchen.

To sum up, creating and cooking meals suitable for an RV requires a thoughtful and flexible approach to cooking while traveling. To maximize the limited resources in an RV kitchen, thoughtful meal planning, effective storage techniques, and the selection of compact kitchen basics are crucial. RV-friendly meals are more convenient and have more variety thanks to adaptable products, inventive cooking methods, and a dedication to flexibility. Travelers may transform the difficulties of RV cooking into chances for culinary creativity and discovery by embracing meal prep, trying out local cuisine, and adopting eco-friendly choices. In the end, developing the skill of meal preparation for an RV makes for a more pleasurable, practical, and tasty road trip experience, where the delights of the adventure continue to the dinner table.

Tips for grocery shopping and storage

Efficient grocery shopping and storage are crucial skills for anyone. Still, they take on a particular significance for those embarking on a road trip, where space is limited, and the availability of grocery stores may vary. This essay aims to provide helpful advice for grocery buying and storage to maximize the enjoyment of the culinary experience while traveling. A well-stocked kitchen and delectable meals throughout the journey may be ensured by following these guidelines, which give practical insights. These tips range from strategic preparation before hitting the road to maximizing storage space within the limits of an RV.

Strategic planning is the cornerstone for storing and shopping for groceries on a road trip. Developing a detailed shopping list before going on the adventure is crucial. This list should be based on the planned meals, and it should consider the kitchen amenities that are accessible in the RV. This list needs to include things that are not only non-perishable but also adaptable, meaning that they may be utilized in various recipes, hence reducing the need for prolonged trips to the grocery store. Additionally, it is recommended to consider the length of the journey and make preparations for perishable foods by that period. It is recommended to select fresh produce with a longer shelf life and to include convenience items requiring less preparation. Additionally, strategic planning not only makes shopping more streamlined but also paves the way for adequate storage and the most effective exploitation of available resources.

When grocery shopping for a road trip, one of the most important considerations is maximizing storage space. A recreational vehicle (RV) has a limited storage capacity, which means that it requires careful organization and the usage of every inch that is accessible. It is possible to make effective use of the space available in cupboards and the pantry by selecting storage containers that are stackable and modular. The correct arrangement of things, the placement of frequently used materials within easy reach, and the organization of storage facilities should all be considered to safeguard against the possibility of spillage or deterioration while traveling. By implementing storage solutions that make the most of vertical space and utilizing the inside of cabinet doors for additional storage pockets, it is possible to significantly increase the overall storage capacity in the RV kitchen.

There is an intelligent method of grocery buying and storing for road trips that involves prioritizing things that can serve several purposes and save space. It is possible to reduce the amount of storage space required while simultaneously increasing the utility that can be achieved by selecting small kitchen basics, collapsible utensils, and flexible gadgets. Portable appliances, such as a tiny blender or a collapsible colander, can perform various functions without wasting valuable storage space. A further factor that contributes to the overall effectiveness of the RV kitchen is the selection of objects that have a dual use, such as a cutting board that can also be used as a container for storage. The ability to strike a balance between functionality and limited storage limits can be achieved by travelers who make strategic selections of products that serve several purposes and save space.

During a road trip, it is possible to avoid overbuying and reduce the amount of food that is wasted by planning meals and making a shopping list that has been well-considered. Travelers can purchase the appropriate quantity of perishable foods by estimating portion sizes and considering the voyage length. This helps to reduce the likelihood that the items would go wrong. In addition, the incorporation of non-perishable essentials with a longer shelf life, such as canned foods, cereals, and pasta, guarantees that a well-stocked pantry is maintained without the concern of items going out of date in a short time. When travelers plan their meals, they can maximize the use of fresh produce by incorporating it into various recipes throughout their trip. This reduces their need to make hurried trips to the grocery store late at night.

Adaptability is one of the most essential qualities to possess when grocery shopping for a road trip. Even though a comprehensive shopping list serves as a guide, visitors should be prepared to make alterations by the availability of things at local stores, seasonal produce, and unexpected culinary ideas. Allowing for flexibility in meal planning and encouraging passengers to visit local markets and specialty stores along the route are two benefits of adopting an adaptable personality. The RV kitchen's versatility extends to food storage since travelers may need to rearrange products to accommodate new purchases or unexpected discoveries. This will ensure that the RV kitchen continues to be well-stocked and diverse.

Convenience products can be of great assistance when it comes to easing the process of grocery shopping and storing groceries when traveling by car. The use of pre-packaged and pre-cut goods, such as salad greens that have already been washed or proteins that have already been marinated, reduces the required preparation and makes the cooking process more efficient. While it is preferable to give fresh and whole meals the highest priority, having a variety of convenience goods in your travel bag is also beneficial to improve both efficiency and convenience. In addition to reducing the time spent in the kitchen, these tools also make the experience of preparing meals on travel more pleasurable and less stressful.

There are opportunities for gastronomic exploration and the discovery of one-of-a-kind regional foods that may be found in the local markets and grocery stores along the journey route. Incorporating excursions to specialized stores or farmer's markets into a traveler's itinerary allows them to interact with the local culinary culture and include particular flavors in their meals. Tourists can learn about the fresh produce, artisanal products, and culinary traditions unique to each destination by making unplanned stops at local markets. While strategic planning is necessary, these trips can teach tourists about these things. Embracing the variety of local products not only improves the overall quality of the culinary experience but also helps sustain the economy of the surrounding areas and leads to a more profound connection with the visited locations.

It is possible to have a more productive and pleasurable experience when cooking in the RV kitchen if the items are well organized and in the appropriate categories. While preparing meals, it is much simpler to locate components if they are arranged in groups similar to one another, such as canned goods, spices, and sauces. Implementing a first-in, first-out method is essential to ensure that perishable commodities are utilized before their expiration dates. Creating storage sections specifically designated for particular kinds of things, such as snacks, essentials for cooking, and fresh fruit, improves organization and accessibility. The pantry and the refrigerator should be well-organized to facilitate the cooking process and contribute to the overall cleanliness of the kitchen space throughout the voyage.

When going grocery shopping for a road trip, environmental considerations like reducing waste and making sustainable choices are essential factors to consider. Choosing to travel with reusable bags, containers, and environmentally friendly kitchen supplies is consistent with a dedication to reducing travel's negative impact on the environment. To lessen the amount of waste produced during the journey, travelers can also prefer products with less packaging or select items that are available in bulk. Contributing to a more sustainable and environmentally conscious approach to road travel is possible by making mindful decisions when shopping for groceries. This type of approach also encourages responsible consumption and waste reduction.

It is a delicate balancing act that involves meticulous preparation of meals and storage strategies to maximize fresh food usage while also limiting wastage. The selection of fruits and vegetables with a longer shelf life, such as apples, oranges, and carrots, guarantees a continuous supply of fresh ingredients throughout the trip. Keeping perishable foods fresher for longer by storing them in vented containers or appropriately producing bags is possible. In addition, travelers can include fresh produce in many meals, ensuring that goods are utilized well before the risk of rotting arises. By giving fresh produce the highest priority, produce and reduce waste, tourists can find a balance between the range of gastronomic options and the convenience of their travels.

It is possible to improve the efficiency of grocery shopping and storage for a road trip by effectively preparing meals in advance. Those who will be traveling can take some time before they wash, cut, and portion up their ingredients so that they will be easier to use while they are on the road. When you prepare marinades, sauces, or spice mixes in advance, you further streamline the cooking process and reduce the time you need to spend in the kitchen. This is especially helpful when traveling in a tight place like an RV. Components that have been well prepared can be stored in resealable bags or compact containers, and they are ready to be utilized for the construction of meals rapidly and efficiently. Travelers can take advantage of the comfort of quick and stress-free cooking while they are on the road if they incorporate meal preparation into their pre-trip routine.

In conclusion, a great road trip gastronomic experience requires efficient grocery shopping and storage, which are crucial components. The overall efficiency of grocery shopping for an RV trip can be improved by practicing strategic planning, making the most of available storage space, prioritizing things that can serve many purposes, and embracing adaptation. When planning a culinary trip, it is essential to take into convenient account goods, to investigate local marketplaces, and to organize everything appropriately. An approach to road travel that is both sustainable and responsible involves several factors, including environmental sensitivity, the reduction of waste, and the maximization of fresh produce. Travelers may ensure they have a well-stocked kitchen, gourmet meals, and an enjoyable culinary adventure during their road trip by being skilled in grocery shopping and storage.

Cooking in the great outdoors

Cooking outside is a gastronomic adventure that blends the tranquility and beauty of nature with the delight of meal preparation. Outdoor cooking provides a special and fulfilling experience, whether backpacking, camping in the woods, or having a picnic in a nearby park. This essay delves into the many facets of cooking outside, encompassing everything from necessary tools and techniques to recipe suggestions and the inextricable bond between food and the environment.

The key to cooking successfully outside is choosing the right tools for the job that fit the environment. Grills, campfires, portable stoves, and small cooking utensils are the components of an outdoor kitchen. The kind of outdoor activity and the resources are major factors in equipment selection. Backpackers may choose small, light cooking equipment, while vehicle campers may get by with a portable grill or stove. Finding a balance between functionality, mobility, and satisfying the gastronomic needs of an outdoor environment is crucial.

A distinctive place in outdoor cooking belongs to campfires, which offer a genuine and traditional way of cooking food and serve as a heat source. Cooking over an open flame gives food a unique flavor and fosters community around the campfire. Cooking over a campfire involves a basic understanding of fire safety, lighting a fire, and using appropriate cookware, like Dutch ovens and cast iron skillets. Campfires may be used for anything from making s'mores to cooking hearty stews, transforming into an adaptable outdoor kitchen that links campers to a long-standing culinary custom.

Using various cooking techniques to suit the outdoor environment is one of the distinguishing characteristics of outdoor cooking. For example, grilling is a common method that gives meats and vegetables a smokey flavor. Portable barbecues provide convenience and versatility. They come in various sizes, from lightweight propane units to compact charcoal grills. Another traditional outdoor cooking technique is Dutch oven cooking, which enables campers to make slow-cooked stews, casseroles, and even desserts. The Dutch oven is a useful equipment for outdoor cooks because of its capacity to transfer heat evenly. Other methods that address various cooking tastes and the limitations of outdoor cookers include steaming, boiling, and foil package cooking.

Cooking outside is more than just preparing food—it's a chance to enhance meals in beautiful, natural settings. Campers can try inventive meals that showcase the tastes of the great outdoors while making the most of scarce ingredients. Easy yet tasty recipes, like foil packet dinners with protein and seasoned veggies, highlight the elegance of simple outdoor cooking. Desserts prepared over a campfire, such as grilled fruit skewers or marshmallow-and-chocolate campfire cones, are a lovely way to cap off an outdoor meal for those with a sweet appetite. These dishes are fun and distinctive because of the rustic appeal of cooking outside and the simplicity of the materials.

When cooking outside, there's a tangible link between food and the environment, which cultivates a profound appreciation for the ingredients and the process of cooking outside. Cooking becomes a multisensory experience when surrounded by natural light, fresh air, and the sounds of nature. The sensory symphony created by the aroma of food blending with the scent of pine trees or the salty sea air enhances outdoor dining. Cooking outdoors becomes a celebration of the senses and a reminder of the connection between people and the environment, whether for breakfast at sunrise, lunch by the trail, or evening beneath the stars.

Cooking outside promotes an intentional approach to obtaining and utilizing food. Campers can consume locally grown food, seasonal veggies, and sustainable protein sources to adhere to ethical and responsible eating. Because of its limited resources, an outdoor kitchen requires more deliberate ingredient selection, raising awareness of food choices' ecological impact. Campers who practice mindfulness also practice waste reduction, bringing reusable containers, packing out rubbish, and reducing the environmental impact of their outdoor cooking.

Cooking outside with friends and family creates a bond and a sense of community among those involved. Whether camping with loved ones, close friends, or other outdoor enthusiasts, cooking and sharing meals becomes a ritual that forges enduring connections. Cooking together over a campfire or communal stove promotes teamwork since everyone pitches in to help prepare the food. Through the thrill of preparing and enjoying delectable meals in the middle of nature, outdoor cooking creates a sense of community and fosters connections.

The importance of safety concerns in outdoor cooking cannot be overstated, as they highlight the necessity of appropriate activities to protect the environment and campers alike. Essential precautions include following fire safety regulations, utilizing approved cooking locations, and handling food properly. Campers should be prepared with basic first aid knowledge and the required equipment to maintain hygienic standards, such as a portable water filtration device. For the sake of future generations, responsible waste disposal techniques like packing out trash and leaving no trace help to maintain the unspoiled beauty of outdoor areas. Making safety and environmental stewardship a top priority turns outdoor cooking into a fun and sustainable pastime.

Regarding outdoor cooking, flexibility is a key characteristic because campers may encounter unforeseen problems like bad weather or scarce supplies. A good outdoor cooking experience involves being adaptable with menu planning, creative with what's on hand, and open to the unexpected. Outdoor chefs that are flexible are better able to deal with shifting circumstances and transform obstacles into chances for creative cooking. Cooking methods are another area where campers must be flexible, as their methods may need to be adjusted in response to equipment limitations and ambient conditions.

Cooking outside is an adventure that is not just reserved for classic camping environments. RV enthusiasts, for instance, can take pleasure in cooking outdoors while enjoying the convenience of a mobile kitchen. RV cooking adds new factors to the mix, like selecting small-space kitchen necessities, adaptable components, and meal planning techniques. The kitchen of an RV transforms into a multipurpose area where a variety of tasty dishes can be prepared, mixing the coziness of home with the thrill of outside discovery. Cooking outside provides a range of opportunities for foodies to enjoy nature's pleasures, whether in an RV, a tent, or over a campfire.

In summary, cooking outside is a dynamic and stimulating beyond simple food preparation. It explores the simplicity and attentiveness of outdoor living, a celebration of nature and a social activity that strengthens bonds between people. By choosing the right tools, embracing various cooking techniques, and creating inventive recipes, outdoor cooking encourages people to interact with their surroundings and recognize the inextricable link between food and the environment. Eating outside becomes a memorable gastronomic experience for individuals who partake in its distinct delights, whether beneath a vast sky, encircled by tall trees, or next to the soothing sounds of the waves.

CHAPTER VII

Connecting with Nature

Hiking trails and outdoor activities

Exploring hiking trails and engaging in outdoor activities form a cornerstone of the human connection with nature, offering many physical, mental, and emotional benefits. Hiking paths offer adventure, physical activity, and a greater understanding of the natural environment. They can range in difficulty from leisurely walks to strenuous hikes. This essay explores the many facets of hiking trails and outdoor pursuits, their importance, the benefits to well-being, proper trail etiquette, and the broader effects of encouraging a love of nature.

Hiking trails are more than routes through the outdoors; they are portals that allow people to experience the peace and beauty of the natural world fully. Hiking paths highlight the extraordinary diversity of our world's landscapes, from lush forests and alpine meadows to coastal cliffs and desert gorges. Hikers can enjoy the fresh, energizing air, the ever-changing landscape, and the sights and sounds of wildlife while hiking these pathways. There are so many hiking paths that one may find something to suit their needs, be it a tough climb for an exhilarating experience, a moderate hike for exercise, or a stroll for introspection.

Hiking, in particular, has been connected to several advantages for physical and mental health when engaging in outdoor activities. Walking and trekking provide a rhythmic action that improves muscle strength, cardiovascular fitness, and endurance in general. Stabilizing muscles are also used when hiking on uneven terrain, which improves balance and coordination. In addition to its health benefits, research indicates that spending time in nature lowers stress, anxiety, and despair. The benefits of being in a natural setting, sometimes known as "ecotherapy" or "green therapy," highlight the significant influence that being outside has on mental health. A sense of peace and mental renewal can be fostered by immersing oneself in a natural setting, away from the daily grind.

Hiking paths also allow people to disconnect from technology and re-establish a connection with the uncomplicated beauty of the outdoors. Hiking becomes a getaway into the sensory richness of the outdoors at a time when electronics and technology rule the world. Hikers are grounded in the present moment by the multisensory experience created by rustling leaves, chattering birds, and pine aroma. Hiking's contemplative qualities promote attention and let people enjoy the sights and sounds of their surroundings without being distracted by the trappings of contemporary life.

Trail etiquette considerations are essential to preserving hiking trails' sustainability and ensuring they are enjoyable for all users. Maintaining these outdoor areas clean and accessible for future generations depends on respecting the environment and other trail users. The idea of "Leave No Trace," which emphasizes reducing one's environmental impact, is one of the cornerstones of trail etiquette. This entails clearing out all rubbish, sticking to authorized pathways, and not upsetting the plants or wildlife. In addition, considerate hikers give way to other trail users, including runners and horseback riders. A peaceful and courteous trail experience is also enhanced by adhering to particular pet behavior rules, such as leash laws and cleaning up after pets. Trail etiquette, which is based on a shared sense of accountability, ensures that everyone can continue enjoying the advantages of hiking paths.

Hiking pathways have benefits beyond personal health and broader environmental preservation and community involvement implications. Hiking routes frequently cross protected natural areas, and using them sensibly helps to keep ecosystems and wildlife intact. Recognizing the value of hiking trails in restoring people's connection to the natural world and instilling a feeling of stewardship, land trusts, conservation organizations, and government agencies work together to create and manage hiking trails. Hiking trail community participation entails locals, outdoor enthusiasts, and organizations cooperating to maintain the trails, promote responsible outdoor recreation, and provide environmental education. People passionate about hiking trails gather together to celebrate the natural world's beauty and make meaningful contributions to its preservation, fostering a feeling of community.

Hiking and other outdoor pursuits open doors to

discovery and adventure, motivating people to stretch their limits and take on new tasks. The variety of hiking paths offers a range of experiences, from strolls appropriate for all ages to challenging excursions that challenge stamina and fortitude. Hikers can select paths that lead to ancient sites, panoramic views, secret alpine lakes, and tumbling waterfalls. Every hiking trail becomes a potential voyage into the unknown when one experiences the joy of exploring new vistas, reaching summits, and negotiating varied terrain.

Engaging in outdoor activities facilitates a more

profound comprehension of the interdependence between the environment and humanity. Due to their admiration for the delicate and stunning natural environments they come across, hikers frequently end up being environmental conservationists. Connecting to nature can make people more conscious of environmental problems, encouraging them to support conservation efforts, adopt sustainable lifestyles, and fight for the preservation of natural areas. Engaging in outdoor activities can help people become environmental ambassadors by converting their passion for hiking trails into a dedication to protecting the earth for the coming generations.

Hiking paths appeal to those seeking physical activity and philosophical and spiritual contemplation. Natural landscapes have spiritual importance acknowledged by many cultures and traditions, which see them as hallowed places that encourage reflection and connection. Hiking trails provide an opportunity for reflection and a way to experience a sense of transcendence because of their meandering routes through mountains, meadows, and forests. The meditative quality of walking enables hikers to transcend the intricacies of everyday existence and fully embrace the splendor and simplicity of the natural world.

Hiking and other outdoor activities allow people to step beyond their comfort zones, develop resilience, and promote self-discovery. Building confidence and tenacity comes from overcoming the physical challenges of a rugged trail or the concerns of navigating uncharted territory. Hikers and outdoor lovers frequently talk about the transformational potential of hiking, citing the enhanced resilience and sense of personal accomplishment that comes from overcoming hurdles on the trail. The life skills gained from hiking trails—such as patience, flexibility, and the capacity to enjoy the journey—go beyond the great outdoors and benefit many facets of daily existence.

In conclusion, outdoor activities and hiking paths signify a deep connection between people and the natural environment beyond simple recreational pastimes. As entry points to various environments, hiking trails provide a range of experiences to suit varying tastes and ability levels. Hiking trails are essential for well-being because they combine the therapeutic benefits of nature with the physical and mental health advantages of outdoor sports. By maintaining these recreational areas sustainably, responsible trail etiquette helps to protect their beauty for both present and future generations. Hiking routes have wider ramifications, such as fostering a stronger bond with nature, community involvement, and environmental protection. Trekking paths provide people with excitement, inspiration, and a deep connection to nature, whether trekking alone for reflection, hiking with friends, or participating in community-driven conservation initiatives.

Wildlife viewing tips

Seeing wildlife is an enthralling and rewarding activity that enables people to connect with the natural world and take in the grace and behavior of various animal species. Whether at a wildlife reserve, a national park, or even someone's backyard, wildlife viewing provides a unique chance to see animals in their native environments. This essay examines essential advice for seeing wildlife, including moral issues, safety measures, and methods to increase the likelihood of seeing wildlife. Wildlife-viewing aficionados must approach the experience with respect, responsibility, and a profound understanding of the fragile balance between people and the animal realm.

Respecting wildlife's boundaries and overall welfare is the cornerstone of ethical wildlife viewing. The idea is to enjoy and observe wildlife without inflicting any harm, stress, or disturbance. Keeping a safe distance is essential since it protects both the viewer and the animals, allowing them to continue their everyday habits. Telephoto lenses and binoculars can be helpful instruments for getting up close without disturbing the animals. It is imperative to repress the urge to approach or feed wild animals because doing so can impede their natural behavior, make them dependent on people, and result in potentially hazardous interactions.

For wildlife viewing to be successful, timing is crucial. Different species display different activity patterns depending on the season, time of day, and weather. The early morning and late afternoon are prime times to see animals because of the milder weather and increased visibility. Planning that works involves thoroughly understanding the target species' unique behaviors and environments. Particular creatures, for instance, are easier to spot close to water sources, while others might be found in thick forests or expansive grasslands. Educating oneself about the habits and inclinations of the target species increases the chances of a satisfying watching encounter.

When it comes to seeing animals, patience is a virtue. Because they don't follow human schedules, animal interactions might be erratic. Finding a peaceful spot to settle in and setting aside time for observation can help you see more of the natural world. This systematic approach also reduces the possibility of upsetting the animals since loud noises or abrupt movements might frighten them and interfere with their routines. When it comes to observing animals, patience is not only a virtue but also a necessary condition for building genuine and lasting relationships with the subjects of the observation.

Silence is a valuable ally when observing wildlife. Numerous animals possess excellent hearing abilities and can discern human presence from a long distance. A less intrusive presence is achieved by moving silently, minimizing loud noises, and having few discussions. Silent observation raises the possibility of picking up on the minute cues of wildlife activity while fully immersing people in the surrounding sounds. The stillness of the natural world helps one become more sensitive to the subtleties of the environment and strengthens one's bond with it.

Understanding the fundamentals of ethical wildlife viewing is beneficial to ecosystems and animal welfare. To limit the biological impact of human presence and prevent habitat destruction, it is imperative to stick to approved paths and observation areas. Aside from causing soil erosion, off-trail activities have the potential to trample vegetation and disturb nesting habitats. Observing the signs and directives issued by conservation authorities guarantees that the animal's natural habitat is not harmed during viewing and contributes to maintaining the sensitive ecosystem's balance. The commitment to responsible wildlife viewing reflects a careful approach to environmental conservation and a determination to protect the areas where wild creatures flourish.

Technology may improve the experience of seeing wildlife when used wisely. Binoculars, cell phones, and cameras are valuable for taking pictures and recording observations. Therefore, these tools must be used about the animals and other onlookers. Switch off phone notifications, turn off security camera sounds, and avoid flash photography since bright lights and loud noises can frighten and disturb wildlife. Technology should enhance the experience rather than diminish it, enabling people to share their findings and advance knowledge and comprehension of the natural world.

People should always be cautious and aware of the possible risks of contact with wild creatures when seeing wildlife. Keeping one's distance is considerate and necessary for one's own security. Even seemingly calm wild animals can act erratically, mainly if they sense danger or are surrounded. Becoming familiar with the unique threats the local wildlife poses is essential. For instance, it's crucial to know the suggested safety precautions in areas where large mammals like bears or big cats are present, such as traveling in groups and carrying bear spray. Being alert, being aware of one's surroundings, and following safety procedures, all help to make seeing animals safe and pleasurable.

It's essential to comprehend the idea of a wildlife "buffer zone" to reduce animal stress and guarantee a secure viewing experience. An imaginary line that people should keep between themselves and wildlife is known as a buffer zone. Species-specific recommendations and guidelines issued by wildlife management agencies determine the appropriate distance. By keeping this buffer zone intact, one is protecting the viewer and the animals, who can act naturally without fear. One of the most important aspects of ethical wildlife viewing is learning to resist the temptation to approach an animal to obtain a better view and realize that animal welfare comes before human desires.

The choice of suitable viewing areas influences the success of wildlife encounters. The likelihood of seeing animals in their natural habitats increases by investigating and selecting locations with wildlife activity. Frequently, dedicated viewing sites and skilled guides in national parks, animal reserves, and designated conservation zones may offer advice on the ideal times and locations for observing wildlife. To improve the overall quality of the wildlife viewing experience, becoming involved with local conservation organizations, naturalist groups, or wildlife experts can provide helpful information on the habitats and behaviors of certain species.

Observing marine and freshwater animals in their native habitats is made possible by aquatic ecosystems, which offer a distinct perspective on wildlife watching beyond terrestrial settings.
It is abundant in biodiversity, providing views of shorebirds, fish species, and marine mammals. Experiences such as kayaking, boat cruises, or just

watching from designated viewing areas can offer a close-up look at aquatic species. Reserving wildlife and its ecosystems depends on responsible behaviors like keeping a safe distance from marine animals and preventing disturbances to nesting locations.

Interaction with nearby communities and indigenous peoples can improve seeing animals in their natural and cultural surroundings. Local knowledge regarding animal behaviors, migration patterns, and the interdependent linkages between animals and the environment is invaluable to understanding the ecosystems under investigation. Learning from indigenous views promotes a comprehensive and courteous approach to animal observation, as these perspectives frequently contain centuries-old understanding about coexisting with wildlife. Supporting regional ecotourism programs and conservation activities also guarantees that the advantages of wildlife viewing reach the residents, who are essential to preserving natural environments.

Observing wildlife is also a type of citizen science in which people provide insightful observations to support scientific studies and conservation initiatives. Through citizen science initiatives and applications for wildlife observation, enthusiasts can record their observations and add them to databases that scientists and conservationists utilize. Wildlife viewing becomes a significant addition to more considerable conservation efforts involving people. Citizen scientists collect data that helps understand animal populations, migration patterns, and the effects of environmental changes. This data is then used to provide essential insights for wildlife conservation.

In summary, seeing animals creates a strong bond between people and the natural world and is an enthralling and life-changing event. The underlying values that direct this connection are a dedication to wildlife protection, ethical behavior, and responsible conduct. Whether they are watching wildlife at a wildlife reserve, a national park, or in their neighborhood, people may positively impact the welfare of wild animals and their environments. Wildlife viewing develops into a shared dedication to preserving the planet's biodiversity and a personal voyage of discovery via tolerance, respect, and a profound understanding of the fragile balance of ecosystems.

Photography and capturing the beauty of National Parks

The fantastic beauty of national parks can be captured and preserved through photography, highlighting the varied landscapes, distinctive ecosystems, and spectacular vistas that characterize these priceless natural gems. Photographers are essential in helping to communicate to a worldwide audience the essence of national parks since they are visual storytellers equipped with cameras. This essay delves into the methodologies, ethical issues, and transforming power of photos in promoting awareness, conservation, and awe for these natural beauties. It also examines the art and relevance of photography in the context of national parks.

With their vast vistas and diverse ecosystems, national parks offer photographers an unmatchedly beautiful canvas. Photographers are presented with various colors, textures, and natural beauties in every park, ranging from majestic mountain ranges and lush forests to tranquil lakes and parched deserts. The difficulty for photographers is condensing these landscapes' breadth and intricacy into a few striking shots that capture the park's essence. To produce photographs that immerse viewers in the heart of these preserved sanctuaries, photographers need to master composition, framing, and light theory.

Beyond merely being technically proficient, the approaches used in national park photography incorporate a profound appreciation for the natural world and a dedication to ethical behaviors. Photographers need help taking striking pictures and causing as minor environmental damage as possible. The Leave No Trace philosophy in national park photography—which emphasizes ethical outdoor practices—resonates strongly. For ethical photographers, it is essential to make sure that their presence disturbs ecosystems, wildlife, and other tourists as little as possible.

For photographers looking to create an engaging visual narrative, comprehending each national park's distinctive features is essential. Photographers can predict the ideal times and locations for shooting classic vistas by researching the park's terrain, weather patterns, and seasonal variations. Photographers who are intimately familiar with the subtleties of a park are better able to capture the soul of that place, whether it be the captivating glow of daybreak on the red cliffs of the Grand Canyon, the mystical mist shrouding Yosemite's waterfalls, or the play of light on Acadia's delicate wildflowers.

A key component of national park photography is light, which affects the pictures' drama, atmosphere, and aesthetic impact. Known as the "golden hours," the gentle tones of dawn or sunset give a warm, charming glow that turns landscapes into dreamy panoramas. Photographs get depth and dimension from the movement of light and shadows during these times, highlighting textures and revealing minute details. Photographers portraying the interaction between light and natural elements frequently use extended exposure techniques. These techniques allow them to depict the movement of clouds, the fluidity of water, or the dancing stars.

In national park photography, the equipment selection is determined by the photographer's vision, the desired result, and the unique obstacles each park presents. While excellent cameras and lenses are necessary to capture clarity and detail, additional equipment like tripods, filters, and drones can be used to increase creative possibilities. Photographers traversing various environments, from muddy marshes to alpine slopes, need lightweight, adaptable equipment. The objective is to keep the agility required to navigate the diverse terrain of national parks while possessing the instruments essential for technical precision.

Photographers in national parks are obligated to communicate the fragility and worth of these ecosystems, acting as stewards in addition to being witnesses to the beauty surrounding them. Photographers minimize their impact on fragile environments and species by following ethical guidelines. Following park restrictions, staying off of trails, and not upsetting wildlife all help preserve the vistas photographers work so hard to capture forever. To keep the park's natural beauty and allow future generations to appreciate its beauty through their own eyes, the main goal is to leave it exactly as discovered.

The potential of photography to arouse feelings, tell tales, and motivate action is what gives it its transformational power. In particular, national park photography is a visual medium for promoting conservation and enjoyment. Through their lenses, photographers take on the role of advocates, stoking wonder, spreading environmental awareness, and convincing people of the need to protect these priceless natural resources. Beyond national borders, the powerful pictures taken in national parks can captivate people and inspire them to appreciate these preserved areas' natural beauty and ecological importance.

Photographers frequently struggle to portray the expanse of national parks in a single shot. Panoramic photography, which enables photographers to combine many photographs to create expansive vistas that capture the grandeur of these natural wonders, becomes an appealing alternative. With the help of panoramas, visitors can get a broad perspective of vast landscapes and fully appreciate the size and grandeur of the park. This method enables photographers to capture the immersive sensation of being in the center of these natural wonders with careful composition and a grasp of the park's geography.

Aerial photography offers a bird's-eye view of the landscapes below, adding a compelling depth to photographs of national parks. Photographers can get novel perspectives and expose patterns, contours, and natural formations that could be obscured from ground-level vantage points by using drones fitted with cameras. Moreover, aerial photography makes it possible to record extensive ecosystems and illustrate the complex interactions between land, water, and plants. But to limit disturbance to wildlife and other tourists, ethical concerns are crucial regarding aerial photography and park regulations and guidelines must be strictly followed.

The advent of social media platforms has wholly changed the photographic environment by making it possible for photographers to share their work with a worldwide audience instantaneously. Photographers and fans of national parks use social media sites like Facebook, Instagram, and Twitter to highlight the beauty of these protected locations. Social media is an effective way to encourage conservation and appreciation, but it also has drawbacks. The chase of the ideal photo, frequently motivated by the need to get likes and shares, might result in excessive site visits, which could adversely affect fragile ecosystems. Responsible photographers use social media to promote moral behavior and environmental care as a tool for activism, education, and inspiration. They also try to find a balance.

Beyond photographing famous scenery, national park photography captures the diverse flora and fauna that call these ecosystems home. Photographers can explore the tiny worlds of national parks through macro photography, which focuses on capturing minute features and patterns. Macro photography reveals the often-overlooked beauty in these natural sanctuaries, from the tiny petals of wildflowers to the exquisite patterns on the wings of butterflies. By allowing viewers to experience the richness of national parks at a microscopic level, this type of photography fosters a closer connection with the complex web of life within these protected regions.

Photographers are presented with a dynamic canvas by the changing seasons in national parks, as each season has its unique color palette and mood. Photographers can capture the ever-changing beauty of these locations in the vivid hues of autumn foliage, the delicate blossoms of spring, the stark contrasts of winter snowscapes, and the green landscapes of summer. Photographers who welcome the seasonal changes in national parks can tell a story through images that go beyond a single frame and highlight the resilience of these ecosystems and the eternal cycles of nature.

To sum up, taking pictures in national parks requires various skills, including a strong understanding of the natural world, moral dilemmas, and the storytelling potential of images. Photographers become national park ambassadors through their lenses, capturing the natural beauty and significance of the environment and transforming the power of these protected areas. The pictures were taken as a link, bringing visitors to the breathtaking.

Marvels of the natural world and encouraging a shared dedication to conservation. As land stewards, photographers are essential to maintaining the allure of national parks for future generations by allowing them to behold and be in awe of the wild beauty that is immortalized via the skill of their cameras.

CHAPTER VIII

Staying Connected on the Road

Communication options for remote areas

As a result of the absence of conventional infrastructure, such as cellular networks and landline connections, communication in remote places provides a unique set of obstacles. On the other hand, technological developments have resulted in the creation of a wide variety of communication choices, enabling individuals to maintain their connection even when they are in the most remote and isolated regions. The purpose of this paper is to investigate a variety of communication solutions that are designed explicitly for distant places. These solutions include satellite communication, radio frequency technologies, and emerging developments such as low Earth orbit (LEO) satellite constellations and mesh networks. In addition to serving practical goals such as emergency circumstances and logistics, the capacity to communicate in remote places helps the well-being and connectivity of communities located in isolated regions and serves valuable purposes.

Regarding facilitating communication in remote locations where there is a lack of terrestrial infrastructure, satellite communication stands out as a fundamental technology. The transmission of signals between ground stations and satellite phones or other communication devices is made possible by satellites that orbit the Earth. This makes it possible to communicate over large distances. It may be economically impossible to establish typical cellular networks in areas with harsh terrain or low population density. Satellite communication is an alternative that can be considered viable in these areas. Users can conduct voice calls, send text messages, and even access rudimentary internet services through satellite phones, which are fitted with antennas that allow them to establish a link with satellites orbiting the Earth. In times of crisis, this technology is quite helpful because it enables people in remote regions to request aid, coordinate rescue activities, or access vital information.

Since long before the introduction of modern digital solutions, radio frequency (RF) technologies have been an indispensable component of communication in geographically isolated regions. Even though they are frequently utilized in aviation, maritime operations, and military situations, high-frequency (HF) and very high-frequency (VHF) radios remain reliable means of communication in regions with limited infrastructure. HF radios, in particular, can cover enormous distances, making them appropriate for long-range communication in geographically isolated areas. Additionally, VHF radios are frequently used for short-range communication in various industries, including search and rescue, forestry, and outdoor recreation. Line-of-sight propagation is the method that these radios use to transmit their signals. While this method can be helpful in environments with little obstructions, it may be challenging to use in regions with dense foliage or mountainous landscapes.

Creating satellite constellations in low Earth orbit (LEO) in distant communication marks a significant and game-changing development. LEO satellites orbit the Earth at lower altitudes than traditional geostationary satellites, which results in reduced signal latency and better communication capabilities. Conventional geostationary satellites orbit the Earth at higher altitudes. SpaceX, OneWeb, and Amazon are among the companies aggressively launching massive constellations of low-Earth orbit satellites to give global broadband internet service, especially in traditionally underserved and remote locations. The purpose of these constellations is to provide people on the ground with access to high-speed internet, thereby bridging the digital divide and opening up new opportunities for communication, education, and economic development in previously isolated areas.

Instead of relying on a central infrastructure, mesh networks provide a decentralized and customizable alternative for communication in remote locations. Mesh networks enable devices to interact with each other rather than relying on their infrastructure. In a mesh network, every device acts as a node capable of transmitting signals to other nodes within the network. This results in the formation of a web of devices that are connected. Implementing this strategy is especially advantageous in regions where establishing conventional communication infrastructure would be either unfeasible or too expensive. Implementing mesh networks is possible through various technologies, such as Bluetooth, Wi-Fi, and custom protocols. Communities located in rural places are given the ability to develop their communication infrastructure through these networks, which helps foster local connectivity and reduces reliance on external providers of telecommunications services.

Drone technology has undergone significant developments in recent years, which has resulted in the introduction of novel communication options in locations that are difficult to reach or distant. To establish temporary communication links, drones equipped with communication relay devices can fly to regions with little or no connectivity. This feature is essential for emergency circumstances because it enables first responders to build communication networks rather quickly. Additionally, drones that are outfitted with payload delivery systems can take communication gear to places that are not easily accessible, helping communities who are in need with either temporary or permanent solutions. Although the adoption of drone-based communication solutions is still in its early phases, there is hope that these solutions will be able to overcome geographical boundaries and improve connectivity in geographically isolated areas.

When providing durable and resilient solutions for

remote places, hybrid techniques that mix different communication technologies are right. A system could incorporate satellite communication for long-distance connection, mesh networks for local communication within a community, and drone-based relays for creating temporary links in challenging terrains. All of these components are considered to be part of the system. To develop a comprehensive communication infrastructure capable of addressing the specific issues associated with remote environments, these hybrid systems make use of each technology's capabilities. These hybrid systems offer a comprehensive approach to communication in locations where traditional options are insufficient. They do this by combining the dependability of satellite communication with the adaptability of mesh networks and the mobility of drones.

Even though these communication choices deliver an

unprecedented level of connectivity to remote locations, a number of issues and considerations need to be addressed to guarantee their efficiency and long-term viability. The expense of building and maintaining satellite communication infrastructure, including ground stations and user devices, can be a considerable obstacle, particularly for communities with few resources. Additionally, governmental permissions, spectrum allocation, and compliance with international agreements are all hurdles that must be overcome for satellite and drone-based communication solutions to be successful. To ensure that these technologies are implemented with respect for local communities and their values, it is necessary to pay close attention to ethical considerations such as concerns over privacy and cultural sensitivities.

Furthermore, conducting a comprehensive analysis of the environmental impact caused by the deployment and maintenance of communication equipment in remote places is essential. This involves determining the amount of carbon dioxide emissions produced by satellite launches, the amount of energy ground stations consume, and the impact drone activities have on the environment. Implementing sustainable practices can reduce the environmental footprint of communication solutions in remote areas. These activities include using renewable energy sources for ground stations and developing environmentally friendly drone technology.

The future holds the potential for even more inventive ways of connecting remote locations since continued advancements in communication technologies are expected to bring about these solutions. Developments in artificial intelligence, machine learning, and edge computing may lead to the creation of communication systems that are more intelligent and will be able to adapt to themselves. In addition, ongoing research in materials science, energy-efficient technologies, and wireless communication may result in advances that improve the efficiency and long-term viability of communication alternatives for outlying regions.

In conclusion, communication in geographically isolated locations has evolved from a complex task into an area that sees fascinating innovation. Several factors, including the convergence of satellite communication, radio frequency technologies, low-Earth orbit satellite constellations, mesh networks, drones, and hybrid techniques, have opened up new horizons for connectivity in previously thought to be isolated areas. These modes of communication make it easier to meet practical requirements like responding to emergencies, managing logistics, and gaining access to information. Still, they also contribute to the overall well-being and connectedness of communities located in remote places. To ensure that communication solutions empower rather than exploit the different landscapes and cultures in remote areas, addressing difficulties and including sustainable practices as technology continues to improve will be essential.

Internet and mobile connectivity tips

In a world that is becoming more interconnected, access to the internet and mobile connectivity has become indispensable for undertaking personal and professional endeavors. Improving internet and mobile connectivity is essential when it comes to keeping informed, productive, and connected with others. This is true whether you are traveling, living in distant places, or navigating daily life in urban environments. This article examines a range of strategies that can be utilized to improve internet and mobile connectivity. These strategies include selecting the appropriate service providers, improving signal strength, monitoring data usage, assuring online security, and using emerging technology. Because of the incorporation of these suggestions, users can maximize their experiences with the internet and mobile devices, regardless of where they are or what their circumstances are.

Selecting the appropriate service provider is essential in guaranteeing dependable connectivity to the internet and mobile devices. Individuals have the luxury of picking based on characteristics such as coverage, speed, and customer service when they live in urban regions, where many providers frequently compete for customers. When individuals conduct research and compare the services offered by various providers, they are better able to make selections that align with their need for connectivity. It is of the utmost importance to select a service provider with the most reach in rural or isolated locations, where coverage may be limited. Some service providers have made it their specialty to assist underdeveloped regions, providing individualized solutions for people who live or travel in rural areas. It is also possible to gain significant insights into the actual performance of a service provider in particular geographic places by considering the input of other users located in the same area.

When improving mobile connectivity, a solid understanding of the available networks and technologies is essential. The degrees of speed and coverage offered by mobile networks of different generations, such as 3G, 4G, and 5G, are differentiated. Rural and distant places may still rely on members of older generations, in contrast to urban areas, which typically have access to the most recent technological advancements. Having knowledge of the leading network technology in a particular region enables consumers to select devices and plans that are compatible with that technology. Additionally, dual-SIM phones that support several network types offer flexibility, allowing customers to move between providers or networks based on their current location and connectivity requirements.

When it comes to maintaining a solid internet and mobile connection, it is essential to maximize signal strength. This is especially true in regions that have rugged terrain or limited infrastructure. Signal reception can be improved by doing uncomplicated activities, such as putting oneself near windows or open areas. External antennas or signal boosters have the potential to significantly improve the signal strength for mobile users, particularly in places that are geographically isolated and have inadequate coverage. Additional factors that can improve connectivity include investing in high-quality equipment, such as routers and modems. When devices are checked regularly for software upgrades, it guarantees that they are equipped with the most recent optimizations and improvements for signal reception.

Exploring alternative technologies could be a game-changer in regions with restricted connectivity alternatives. The use of satellite internet, for instance, provides a workable alternative for people who live in rural areas where regular wired or cellular networks are not available. Even though satellite internet has traditionally been plagued by issues such as high latency and elevated costs, technological improvements have resulted in choices that are both more accessible and more reliable. Satellite constellations have been launched by companies such as SpaceX's Starlink to provide internet access worldwide. This is especially beneficial for customers who live in rural and economically disadvantaged areas. Individuals can select the solution that is most suitable for their particular connectivity requirements when they have a thorough understanding of the capabilities and drawbacks of various technologies.

Controlling the amount of data used is extremely important, particularly for people who rely on mobile data plans with restrictions. Monitoring data use eliminates the possibility of incurring charges that were not anticipated and guarantees that connectivity will be available throughout the billing cycle. Activating data-saving capabilities on devices and applications can assist in optimizing usage without compromising the essential functionality. Preloading maps, articles, or other content, while connected to Wi-Fi, can offer access even when internet connectivity is irregular in distant places with poor data coverage. This is especially useful in situations where there is little data coverage. In addition, the utilization of compression tools or lightweight versions of applications helps conserve bandwidth, thereby maximizing the available data allotment.

Because consumers access various services and sensitive information, ensuring online security is essential to internet and mobile connectivity. This is especially true in instances where individuals access the internet. The use of safe and unique passwords for each account, the use of two-factor authentication, and the routine updating of software and firmware on devices all contribute to a solid security posture. Individuals must exercise caution and use virtual private networks (VPNs) when connecting to public Wi-Fi networks. This will allow them to encrypt their internet traffic and protect themselves from potential risks. It is essential to thoroughly understand the privacy settings on your devices and applications to provide an additional layer of security and guarantee that your personal information is kept safe.

The utilization of developing technologies has the potential to offer individuals novel solutions to problems associated with connectivity constraints. Mesh networks, for example, enable devices to connect, establishing a decentralized network that does not necessarily rely on a centralized infrastructure. This strategy is beneficial in geographically isolated locations and where it would be impractical to develop conventional communication infrastructure. Communities can establish their own local networks through mesh networks, which helps foster connectivity even in the absence of traditional service providers. Artificial intelligence and machine learning in connection solutions can improve the user experience by optimizing network performance, predicting connectivity issues, and adapting to changing conditions. In the end, this will result in an improved user experience.

For efficient connectivity, it is essential to have a solid understanding of the particular challenges that a specific place presents. Both the signal's strength and the network's performance can be affected by various factors, including topography, weather conditions, and the density of obstructions such as buildings or vegetation. Individuals can modify their approach to address unique difficulties by conducting site surveys and considering the physical environment when creating connectivity solutions. When overcoming environmental constraints and increasing connectivity, there are certain situations where making minor alterations, such as repositioning a router or utilizing directional antennas, can make a significant difference.

Individuals can gain valuable insights into the operation of their connection solutions by maintaining a regular testing schedule for their internet and mobile services. Users can evaluate download and upload speeds, as well as latency, through various internet tools and mobile applications. Conducting speed tests at different times of the day and under varied conditions helps uncover patterns and potential problems. This allows for proactive steps to be taken to enhance connectivity efficiency. Getting in touch with the service provider for assistance or troubleshooting on the network configuration might help address the underlying issues and improve overall performance if consistent connectivity problems continue.

When it comes to improving connection, community engagement is of the utmost importance, particularly in more rural locations where traditional infrastructure may be missing. The formation of local initiatives or cooperatives allows community members to combine their resources, increase their skills, and work together to overcome difficulties related to connection. Establishing community networks, shared access points, and cooperative investments in infrastructure are all possibilities that might be included in this collaborative approach. To develop a sense of empowerment and self-reliance among its members, communities can create resilient and sustainable connection solutions by working together. These solutions will benefit all members of the community.

The optimization of internet and mobile connectivity is a complicated endeavor that demands a mix of intelligent choices, technological understanding, and adaptability. In conclusion, this endeavor requires a combination of these three factors. Individuals can improve their connectivity in urban environments as well as in remote areas by selecting the appropriate service providers, gaining an understanding of the available networks, maximizing the strength of the signal, managing the amount of data they use, ensuring that they are secure online, utilizing emerging technologies, and working together with communities. In an era in which connectivity is synonymous with opportunities and knowledge, these suggestions equip individuals with the ability to traverse the intricacies of the digital landscape and make the most of their interactions with the internet and mobile devices.

Balancing technology and nature

The junction of technology and the environment is a crucial juncture in the ever-changing landscape of the 21st century, and it requires careful analysis and intelligent navigation to navigate it successfully. The delicate nature of humanity's symbiotic interaction with the natural world is becoming more apparent as the human race embraces the marvels introduced by technological advancement. Pursuing a peaceful equilibrium between the two realms is not only a philosophical problem; it is a practical necessity for advancing our planet toward a more sustainable future.

Without a doubt, the world we live in has been transformed by technology, which has experienced exponential growth and can transform. From the industrial revolution to the digital age, every innovation has brought about changes in our way of life, how we work, and how we communicate with one another that has never been seen before. However, the quick speed of technological innovation has not been without drawbacks, and it has frequently left a trail of environmental devastation in its wake. The pursuit of convenience and progress has destroyed forests, caused the emission of harmful pollutants, and accelerated climate change. These factors pose enormous dangers to the delicate balance of ecosystems worldwide.

The urge to reestablish a connection with the natural world is becoming more pressing than ever amid the rapid advancement of technology. In the process of urbanization spreading its concrete tendrils across landscapes, there is an increasing disconnect between individuals and the natural environment. This disconnection not only jeopardizes the well-being of individuals but also diminishes the value that biodiversity possesses in and of itself. There is a growing movement to incorporate nature into the fabric of our technological civilization, which is a response to the significant impact of this disconnection.

An approach to architecture known as "biophilic design," founded on the notion that people have a natural affinity for the natural world, aims to incorporate elements of the natural world into the constructed environment. It is becoming increasingly common for architects and urban planners to incorporate green spaces, natural light, and sustainable materials into their designs. This helps to cultivate a sense of connectedness with the natural world. Not only can the deliberate incorporation of natural elements into urban areas boost the aesthetic appeal of these areas, but it also contributes to enhancing mental health and overall well-being.

In addition, the development of environmentally friendly technologies shows a glimmer of hope for a more sustainable future. One of the most critical steps we can take is to harness the power of renewable energy sources like solar and wind to lessen our reliance on fossil fuels and lessen the impact of climate change. By minimizing ecological footprints and fostering responsible resource management, sustainable practices in agriculture and industry provide the potential to encourage accountable resource management. These methods are guided by technical innovation. We can pave the way for a future in which technology and nature may coexist in a mutually beneficial way if we choose these environmentally responsible options.

However, a nuanced approach is necessary because the delicate tango between technology and the environment necessitates it. If they are not utilized responsibly, technical breakthroughs that hold the key to environmental sustainability can also be a double-edged sword. The methods that are both ethical and sustainable need to be used to put a stop to the widespread exploitation of natural resources that is being done in the name of technological advancement. A paradigm shift in our innovation approach is required to meet the challenge of striking a balance. This shift should place an emphasis not only on efficiency and profit but also on environmental stewardship.

Education is one of the most critical factors when cultivating a culture of responsible technological growth. Understanding the complex web of life and the impact of human actions on the world can be accomplished by incorporating environmental studies into the curriculum at all levels. The next generation of innovators can be inspired to emphasize sustainability in their undertakings if they are allowed to cultivate a sense of ecological consciousness. Through the instillation of a profound reverence for the natural world, education transforms into a catalyst for change, guiding humanity towards a future in which technology enhances rather than abuses the natural environment.

Biomimicry is a concept that shows the potential for technology to gain inspiration from the ingenuity found in nature. Engineers and designers can develop solutions that are not only technologically advanced but also environmentally friendly if they model their work after the efficiency and elegance of natural systems. Biomimicry provides a blueprint for a harmonious cohabitation between technology and nature. This blueprint incorporates a variety of technologies, such as Velcro, which was inspired by the mechanism of burdock burrs, and energy-efficient buildings that are modeled after termite mounds.

Nevertheless, as we traverse this complex equilibrium, it is essential to acknowledge the socio-economic aspects of the equation. To create inclusivity and move forward progress, having access to technology has the potential to empower communities and bridge divisions. The proliferation of digital technologies in healthcare, education, and communication has the potential to elevate societies and improve the quality of life for millions of people. A holistic approach that considers the interconnection of social, economic, and ecological systems is required to strike a balance between these positive consequences and the requirement of taking measures to preserve the environment.

In conclusion, the delicate tango between technology and nature is a problem that stands out as characterizing our time. At this juncture, where we find ourselves at the intersection between progress and preservation, it is essential to recognize the complex relationship between the two spheres. The route forward rests in the integration of technology and nature in a conscientious manner, wherein innovation is balanced by ecological responsibility. By cultivating a profound connection with the natural world, adopting environmentally responsible habits, and using technology to effect positive change, we can strive for a future in which humanity flourishes in harmony with the planet. Striking a balance between the demands of technology and the needs of nature is not merely a matter of personal preference; instead, it is a shared responsibility that will determine the legacy we leave for future generations.

CONCLUSION

In the pages of "Beyond the Campfire: Rving in National Parks Made Easy - A Traveler's Handbook for Unforgettable Adventures," readers embark on a journey that transcends the ordinary, offering a comprehensive guide to unlocking the full potential of RV travel within the breathtaking landscapes of national parks. As the final chapter unfolds, it becomes evident that this e- book is more than just a travel guide; it is a portal to a world of unparalleled exploration and connection with nature.

The central theme of the book revolves around the

seamless integration of technology and nature, exemplifying the delicate balance discussed throughout this work. The handbook not only serves as a practical guide for RV enthusiasts, detailing tips and tricks for navigating the intricacies of national park visits, but it also emphasizes the importance of responsible and sustainable travel. By promoting eco-friendly practices and encouraging readers to tread lightly on the natural wonders they encounter, "Beyond the Campfire" aligns itself with the broader conversation about balancing technology and nature.

The concluding chapters leave readers inspired and

equipped, not only with practical knowledge but also with a profound appreciation for the beauty and fragility of the environments they are poised to explore. The call to action echoes throughout the e-book, urging travelers to embrace a mindset that goes beyond the mere thrill of adventure, fostering a deep respect for the sanctity of the national parks and the ecosystems they harbor.

As the virtual pages close, readers are left with more

than just a handbook—they have a companion for their journeys, a source of inspiration, and a guide to cultivating unforgettable memories. "Beyond the

Campfire" serves as a testament to the idea that technology and nature need not be at odds; instead, they can coexist harmoniously to enhance our experiences and deepen our connection with the natural world. This e-book is an invaluable resource for anyone seeking to embark on an RV adventure, providing not only the tools for a successful trip but also the wisdom to tread responsibly on the path less traveled.

Thank you for buying and reading/listening to our book. If you found this book useful/helpful please take a few minutes and leave a review on the platform where you purchased our book. Your feedback matters greatly to us.